New Daylight

Edited by Naomi Starkey   January–April 2003

Suggestions for using New Daylight

Set aside a regular time and place, if possible, when you can read and pray undisturbed. Before you begin, take time to be still and, if you find it helpful, use the BRF prayer. Read the Bible passage slowly—if the passage is over familiar, try reading it aloud for a change—and then turn to the comment.

The prayer, question or point for reflection can be a starting point for your own meditation and prayers. You may find it helpful to keep a journal to record your thoughts about the passage or comment, or to note items for prayer. Another way of using New Daylight is to meet with others to discuss the material, either regularly or occasionally.

In New Daylight the Sundays and special festivals from the Church calendar are noted on the relevant days. This offers a chance to recall or get acquainted with the rich traditions of the Christian year.

Writers in this issue

Rob Gillion is Vicar of Upper Chelsea, London, and Evangelism Adviser for the Bishop of Kensington. He broadcasts regularly both nationally and locally, including BBC Radio's 'Pause for Thought'. He was formerly a parish priest and prison chaplain in Hong Kong.

Helen Julian CSF is an Anglican Franciscan sister, a member of the Community of St Francis, and presently Guardian of St Francis Convent, Compton Durville, in Somerset. She has written *Living the Gospel* for BRF.

Adrian Plass is an internationally popular writer and speaker in many countries. His most recent book for BRF is *When You Walk*.

Colin Evans is a former Moderator of the Eastern Province of the United Reformed Church, writer and broadcaster. He lives near Sudbury, in Suffolk.

Rachel Boulding is Deputy Editor of the *Church Times*. For some years she was Senior Editor at SPCK Publishing, commissioning religious books. She lives with her husband and young son in Dorset.

Christine Chapman was Director of Counselling for the Chester diocese. She is currently a member of the North-West Inter-Diocesan Counselling Team for clergy and their families, and is a lay Reader in her church.

Margaret Cundiff has worked in the Church of England since 1973, as a lay worker, deaconess, deacon and finally priest. She also broadcasts regularly and serves as Diocesan Mothers' Union Chaplain in the York Diocese. Her most recent book for BRF is *Still Time for Eternity*.

Jenny Robertson lived for a number of years in Russia, working alongside her husband in St Petersburg. She has written many books for both adults and children, including *Windows to Eternity* and *Strength of the Hills* for BRF. She has also had a number of books of poetry published.

David Winter is retired from parish ministry. An honorary Canon of Christ Church, Oxford, he is well known as a writer and broadcaster. He is the author of BRF's Lent book for 2002, *With Jesus in the Upper Room*. He is a Series Editor of *The People's Bible Commentary*.

David Spriggs is a Baptist minister, currently working as Head of Church Relations for Bible Society, where he had also been Project Director for The Open Book.

Naomi Starkey writes...

More and more people are aware these days that the Bible is more like a library than a single book, and there has been an increasing appreciation of the different types of literature found in the Bible. We have everything from military history to love poetry, and some of it (genealogies, for example) are—to put it mildly—hard to read devotionally.

I am a strong believer in considering the Bible as a whole, as well as in its individual parts. We have the whole of Scripture to consider when we think about our faith and about our God, and we can't leave some parts on one side because we don't immediately see how they relate to us.

The challenge for the *New Daylight* editor is to find ways of covering the different types of biblical literature in a daily readings format. Not every book works on a verse-by-verse basis, and unless we find a variety of approaches, we can end up ignoring swathes of Scripture, especially in the Old Testament—which was the whole of Scripture as far as Jesus and the early Church were concerned.

In commissioning *New Daylight*, I ask for the verse-by-verse method, but also for thematic approaches, book over-views, and character studies. Some contributors also supply 'further reading' suggestions, to help provide context for the passage being studied. A book overview (as David Winter wrote on Numbers for the September 2002 issue) can be an excellent way of getting to know an unfamiliar part of the Bible, and (I hope) tempting the reader to further study, perhaps using one of BRF's *People's Bible Commentary* titles.

Thematic approaches (the writer choosing both Old and New Testament material to illustrate the subject) can show how the message of the whole Bible fits together. Occasionally this can lead to two writers commenting on the same passage, quite by chance, but that is a fine illustration of how more than one lesson can be drawn from the same part of the Bible.

In our Scripture reading we can return to favourite passages and find fresh insights because we are reading with fresh eyes, our own circumstances having changed in some way. And we can also find that books or passages that at one stage seemed quite dry and dull can become the very place where we hear God speaking most clearly. We just need to be ready to listen!

The BRF Prayer

Almighty God,
you have taught us that your word is a lamp for our feet
and a light for our path. Help us, and all who prayerfully
read your word, to deepen our fellowship with each other
through your love. And in so doing may we come to know you
more fully, love you more truly, and follow more faithfully in
the steps of your son Jesus Christ, who lives and reigns with
you and the Holy Spirit, one God for evermore. Amen.

Joshua 1—6

The character of Joshua highlights the themes of his book. It is a book full of challenges faced by Joshua and his people, but also challenges for ourselves. The death of Moses signals the end of one journey and the beginning of another. It is Joshua's role to lead the people through a transition to a new era. If Joshua is to lead his people effectively, he needs to be strong and very courageous. He needs to be obedient, not afraid, and not get confused. Joshua's leadership shows that there are times of great decisiveness, but also times when he is well prepared one moment and not having a clue the next! He combines success with disappointment. Although, as we shall read, he leads his people with mixed results, he remains faithful to God and serves his people.

Joshua has, it seems, been in Moses' shadow, appearing timid and uncertain. The first words that Moses hears from God about Joshua are 'encourage and strengthen him' (Deuteronomy 3:28). After Moses' death, God tells Joshua three times 'Be strong and courageous' (Joshua 1:7ff). As Joshua walks alone, around the walls of Jericho, he is reminded that God is the true commander of the troops. It looks as if the greatest of all Joshua's victories was over his own temperament. For meek souls that is always important.

I suppose the reason I am so excited about writing some notes on these first six chapters is that I see much of how my ministry has unfolded. For many years I have felt somewhat second class as a Christian, and I have seen great giants of faith who have reminded me of Moses. God has had his work cut out assuring me that, actually, I'm OK! He knows my strengths and weaknesses and is quite prepared to work with me.

I pray that, as we share this time together, you will journey with Joshua with the assurance of the promises of God in the challenges you face on your journey of life.

Rob Gillion

Promises, promises

After the death of Moses the servant of the Lord, the Lord said to Joshua son of Nun, Moses' assistant: 'Moses my servant is dead. Now then, you and all these people, get ready to cross the Jordan River into the land I am about to give to them—to the Israelites. I will give you every place where you set your foot, as I promised Moses. Your territory will extend from the desert to Lebanon, and from the great river, the Euphrates—all the Hittite country—to the Great Sea on the west. No one will be able to stand up against you all the days of your life. As I was with Moses, so I will be with you; I will never leave you nor forsake you.'

Moses has brought the Israelites to the edge of the Promised Land. Now Joshua is to be the one to lead them into the 'land of milk and honey'. His joy is to be found in the role of the one who consolidates all that Moses has achieved. Perhaps there was a hint of disappointment for Moses—after all he was only human. He would have rejoiced, though, in the fact that his part of the journey, tough and difficult as it had been, had not been in vain. He was the right person for that hazardous journey through the wilderness, with such love for God and his people.

Some are called to be pioneers, others to build on the foundations laid by others. When things were not going according to plan, the people were quick to blame God, but, so often, when things were going well, they took the credit and forgot to give God thanks and praise. It was Joshua's task to remind them constantly how much God had done for them and that they were to be obedient.

In the sacrament of marriage, the vows made are the same as those we should make to God— 'for better for worse, for richer for poorer, in sickness and in health'. This is only right, for God said, 'As I was with Moses, so I will be with you; I will never leave you nor forsake you.' Now there's a promise!

Thanksgiving

Guide me, O thou great Redeemer,
Pilgrim through this barren land;
I am weak but thou art mighty;
Hold me with thy powerful hand.

W. Williams (1717–91)
RobG

Love, cherish and obey

'Be strong and courageous, because you will lead these people to inherit the land I swore to their forefathers to give them. Be strong and very courageous. Be careful to obey all the law my servant Moses gave you; do not turn from it to the right or to the left, that you may be successful wherever you go. Do not let this Book of the Law depart from your mouth; meditate on it day and night, so that you may be careful to do everything that is written in it. Then you will be prosperous and successful. Have I not commanded you? Be strong and courageous. Do not be terrified; do not be discouraged, for the Lord your God will be with you wherever you go.'

Time and time again the scriptures speak of 'righteousness', meaning a proper relationship between God and the community of God's people. Once again, the promises we make in our marriage vows apply to our relationship with God—we should promise to 'love, cherish and obey'. To do so connects with the calling to us to be disciples. Many were known to be followers of Jesus, but only a few were true disciples. In these few verses, being strong and courageous are the virtues that God commends. So often I think I have to act in my own strength, but I can't. I must rely on his strength and then my courage is well founded. God is reminding his people that whenever they decide to take things into their own hands, disaster strikes.

It's no coincidence that Joshua is the man given this task of reminding the Israelites of their allegiance and obedience to God. His revelation is found in reading and meditating on the Book of the Law, handed down from God through Moses; ours comes via Jesus himself. Joshua is the same name as Jesus and means the fulfilment of all history. As Peter so wonderfully expresses it when he is asked by Jesus whether or not they want to continue to follow as disciples, 'Lord, to whom else shall we go? You have the words of eternal life' (John 6:68). We have this word revealed in scripture and made flesh in Christ himself, with the strength of the Holy Spirit.

Song

'Be bold, be strong, for the Lord your God is with you'. Sing, doing the actions, too, if you know them!

ROBG

Divided we fall

So Joshua ordered the officers of the people: 'Go through the camp and tell the people, "Get your supplies ready. Three days from now you will cross the Jordan here to go in and take possession of the land the Lord your God is giving you for your own."'

In order to cross the river, a number of challenges have to be overcome, the greatest of these being that of maintaining unity. I have often wondered why companies send their employees off on courses to build bridges and climb mountains. What help is that in running a bank, managing a department store or whatever? Here is the answer—to achieve a goal with a team there needs to be a unity of purpose and that is useful in any endeavour.

Here Joshua is faced with the challenge of claiming the territory he has been promised, but the tribes will be divided by the river. His task is to get the eastern tribes to help him before they get too settled. Moses had already foreseen this difficulty, so Joshua is able to remind them of the promises they gave to Moses (Numbers 32:25–27). Obviously Moses was held in very high esteem, so Joshua was able to build on the goodwill that had been engendered.

When I worked in Hong Kong as a priest and pastor, I was so impressed with the Chinese churches in Hong Kong. Whenever there was a need to plant a new church, all the other churches in the diocese would rally round and help. There was no sense of 'only in my back yard', but a genuine feeling that we were all in mission together. Obviously that idea had been well defined in the case of Joshua for the eastern tribes were very happy to come to the aid of their western brothers and sisters (vv. 16–17). This always remains a vital task for the people of God. In our present world, where there is so much disunity, here is a situation where God unites divided forces to focus on the task in hand.

Prayer

Almighty God, who hast given us grace at this time with one accord to make our common supplications unto thee… Fulfil now, O Lord, the desires and petitions of thy servants, as may be most expedient for them.
Amen

Prayer of St Chrysostom
*ROB*G

Rahab and the spies

Then Joshua son of Nun secretly sent two spies... 'Go, look over the land,' he said, 'especially Jericho.' So they went and entered the house of a prostitute named Rahab and stayed there. The king of Jericho was told, 'Look! Some of the Israelites have come here tonight to spy out the land.' So the king of Jericho sent this message to Rahab: 'Bring out the men who... entered your house, because they have come to spy out the whole land.' But the woman had taken the two men and hidden them. She said, 'Yes, the men came to me, but I did not know where they had come from. At dusk, when it was time to close the city gate, the men left. I don't know which way they went...'

As the narrative leads us closer to the Promised Land, we note that Joshua, being new to leadership, is determined not to make any mistakes. God told Joshua to cross the Jordan, but he is not quite convinced that he has heard him correctly. So, he sends out spies to gather intelligence. By doing so he loses the element of surprise and almost fails before he has started.

I shall never forget my first experience of teaching in a strange land. I was invited to teach mime in Norwich Prison. I had had quite a lot of experience of performing, but not so much of teaching. I arrived at the prison and was faced with what I thought was a hostile audience. So I started to tell them what I was going to do. I told them about my experience as a performer. Then I started to explain the outline of the session. After about 15 minutes of explaining, an inmate said, 'Excuse me, I know you're nervous, but when are we actually going to do any mime?' It was just what I needed.

It is so easy to be nervous about making decisions when you are in a new role. Joshua had been well trained for leadership by Moses. He trusted in God's promises that he would lead the Israelites into Canaan successfully. Just as it was a prisoner who came to my aid, a most unlikely ally, so God sends Rahab the prostitute to Joshua to bail him out.

Reflection

God moves in a mysterious way!

ROBG

A land of promises

'Please swear to me by the Lord that you will show kindness to my family, because I have shown kindness to you…' 'Our lives for your lives!' the men assured her. 'If you don't tell what we are doing, we will treat you kindly and faithfully…' So she [Rahab] let them down by a rope through the window for the house she lived in was part of the city wall. Now she had said to them, 'Go to the hills so that the pursuers will not find you. Hide yourselves there three days until they return, and then go your way.' The men said to her, 'This oath you made us swear will not be binding on us unless, when we enter the land, you have tied this scarlet cord in the window…'

This exciting tale continues to remind us how much God enjoys faithfulness, and how we disappoint him when we do not trust him. Joshua and his spies learned a valuable lesson. Here Rahab—representing a disreputable profession with marginal social status, seemingly of no consequence—handles the situation with calmness and authority. This young woman asks not for financial reward or safety for herself, but that her family should be saved. Here is selflessness that is well rewarded.

The spies then tell her what to do to save her life and the lives of her family—tie a scarlet cord in the window when the tribes attack the city. Early Church leaders suggested that we should associate the cord with the blood of Jesus. They taught that just as the cord saved the lives of Rahab and her family, so the blood of Christ saved us. I'm not sure that we can read as much as that into this event. I see much more resonance with how Jesus treated women, especially those who were not to be spoken to or associated with. Here we have a non-Israelite outsider entering God's kingdom by means of her faithfulness. This part of the story, which focuses so particularly on Rahab, may also be told to explain why a Canaanite woman appears in the family tree of David and, eventually, the ancestry of Joseph of Nazareth (Matthew 1:5).

Sunday reflection

'Do not let your hearts be troubled. Trust in God…' (John 14.1).

ROBG

Crossing the Jordan

Early in the morning Joshua and all the Israelites set out from Shittim and went to the Jordan, where they camped before crossing over. After three days the officers went throughout the camp, giving orders to the people: 'When you see the ark of the covenant of the Lord your God, and the priests, who are Levites, carrying it, you are to move out from your positions and follow it. Then you will know which way to go, since you have never been this way before. But keep a distance of about a thousand yards between you and the ark; do not go near it.' ... As soon as the priests who carried the ark reached the Jordan... the water from upstream stopped flowing... So the people crossed over opposite Jericho... on dry ground.

We need to catch our breath after the excitement of the previous chapter! Everyone is raring to go, to enter the Promised Land at last, but Joshua knows just how important this crossing is to his people. So, he repeats commands and each event is described in meticulous detail (do read the whole chapter to get the full account). It is not just an historical event for the people of that time and in that place, but also a drama—a constant reminder to future generations of the loving promises of God. There is the powerful symbol of the ark showing the people the way to go—God as the supreme commander leading Israel. The people are instructed to walk half a mile behind as a mark of respect.

The River Jordan is crossed by a miracle, echoing the crossing of the Red Sea at the start of the Exodus. Once again it is a way in which God lets his people know that none of their clever intelligence networks or their best-laid plans will amount to much if they operate with little reference to God and his mighty acts. Without the river parting miraculously, they could not have continued their journey; without the faith of Rahab, they would have failed. The greatest partnership we have is with God.

Reflection

'The Lord is my shepherd, I shall not be in want. He makes me lie down in green pastures, he leads me beside quiet waters' (Psalm 23:1–2).

ROBG

JOSHUA 4:1–7 (NIV, ABRIDGED)

Memorials

When the whole nation had finished crossing the Jordan, the Lord said to Joshua, 'Choose twelve men from among the people, one from each tribe, and tell them to take up twelve stones from the middle of the Jordan... and to carry them over with you and put them down at the place where you stay tonight... to serve as a sign among you. In the future, when your children ask you, "What do these stones mean?", tell them that the flow of the Jordan was cut off before the ark of the covenant of the Lord. When it crossed the Jordan, the waters of the Jordan were cut off. These stones are to be a memorial to the people of Israel forever.'

When we were living in Norfolk, we used to have family membership of the National Trust. We lived very close to Blickling Hall and used to enjoy visiting the gardens. Our children were very young and there was a 'secret garden' that they discovered, guarded by a stone dog. We never found anyone who could tell us his story, so we had to use our imaginations. I remember my older boy turning to the younger and saying, 'If only the dog could talk!' Here in this story the stones do talk. They were used as an object lesson, a powerful teaching tool for future generations. In every age, the people of God have tangible reminders of the Lord's guidance and deliverance, ones that serve as reminders for generations to come—much more solid than a knot in a handkerchief.

The people in the passage had an obligation to explain the special events to their children and their significance. This points up a possible strategy for evangelism—utilizing the significance of memorial and remembrance to help us not forget what God has done for us. These 12 stones remind us of his saving grace and his promise fulfilled. Immediately, too, my imagination takes me to an upper room with 12 disciples and Christ's promise to them: they are to be living stones (1 Peter 2:4), proclaiming the good news of Christ.

Reflection

A perfect memory of his death and passion until his coming again.

Book of Common Prayer
ROBG

Home sweet home

The Lord said to Joshua 'Make flint knives and circumcise the Israelites again'... Now this is why he did so: All those who came out of Egypt—all the men of military age—died in the desert on the way after leaving Egypt. All the people that came out had been circumcised, but all the people born in the desert during the journey from Egypt had not... And after the whole nation had been circumcised, they remained where they were in camp until they were healed... On the evening of the fourteenth day of the month... the Israelites celebrated the Passover. The day after the Passover... they ate some of the produce of the land: unleavened bread and roasted grain... There was no longer any manna for the Israelites, but that year they ate of the produce of Canaan.

When we read the adventures in the wilderness, we see that the Israelites were sometimes forgetful people. Again and again they either rebel against God or forget him—usually at a time when they have 'never had it so good.' Moses had a difficult task on his hands to ensure that they remained God's people.

Circumcision, though not an appealing thought, it is a permanent reminder of who they are—the chosen people. It also represents an outward sign of an inward condition, just as baptism signals a change of heart for the Christian. Here it signalled the promise to a new generation, that they must not forget who they are and the importance of their homecoming.

In the prison where I worked as chaplain, the most valued possession of those prisoners who were baptized in prison was the small wooden cross that they received. They wore it around their neck and never took it off.

The final action of this passage also signals a new beginning as the people eat food grown in Canaan—not manna from heaven, but home-baked bread. Once again, my thoughts leap to the upper room. The Passover meal celebrated a new beginning as Jesus was no longer going to be present physically to help them. God was in the process of building effective disciples, not feeding dependent disciples.

Reflection

'You did not choose me, but I chose you and appointed you to go and bear fruit—fruit that will last'
(John 15:16).

ROBG

Moses' look-alike

Now when Joshua was near Jericho, he looked up and saw a man standing in front of him with a drawn sword in his hand. Joshua went up to him and asked, 'Are you for us or for our enemies?' 'Neither,' he replied, 'but as commander of the army of the Lord I have now come.' Then Joshua fell face down to the ground in reverence, and asked him, 'What message does my Lord have for his servant?' The commander of the Lord's army replied, 'Take off your sandals, for the place where you are standing is holy.' And Joshua did so.

This encounter parallels Moses' experience with the burning bush (Exodus 3:5). God told Moses that he was standing on holy ground and should take off his sandals. The warrior angel asks Joshua to do the same. It was so difficult to step into the shoes of the great prophet Moses, and he may have been anxious that he would never match up. Here was a tremendous affirmation—similar sandals to remove and holy ground to step on!

Whenever I speak of holiness, I become aware of the infinite difference between God and human beings. It is a reminder of the need for reverence. Of course there is the intimacy shared in my relationship with Christ, but there is also the awesomeness of God. It is so tempting when given an awesome responsibility to either believe that you must be awesome, too, or find it all so overwhelming that you cannot take the next step.

Whichever thoughts or feelings Joshua was having, this messenger reminded him of who was in charge. Right at the outset he is reminded that God doesn't take sides. He responds favourably to those who are obedient in love towards him. When asked, 'Are you for us or for our enemies?' the angel replies 'Neither'. It is comforting that the heavenly commander is there, but disturbing to know that he may change sides in any conflict. Either answer undermines any idea of a holy war. God does not fight for a chosen nation but remains independent from any persuasion or ritual or appeasement. He responds only to obedience and righteousness.

Reflection
'Seek ye first the kingdom of God, and his righteousness'
(Matthew 6:33, AV).

RobG

Battle stations

Now Jericho was tightly shut up because of the Israelites... Then the Lord said to Joshua, 'See, I have delivered Jericho into your hands, along with its king and its fighting men. March around the city once with all the armed men. Do this for six days. Make seven priests carry trumpets of rams' horns in front of the ark. On the seventh day, march around the city seven times, with the priests blowing the trumpets. When you hear them sound a long blast on the trumpets, make all the people give a loud shout; then the wall of the city will collapse and the people will go up, every man straight in.' So Joshua son of Nun called the priests and said to them, 'Take up the ark of the covenant of the Lord and make seven priests carry trumpets in front of it.' And he ordered the people, 'Advance! March around the city, with the armed guard going ahead of the ark of the Lord.'

Here is a typical promise of victory that motivates Joshua's troops. It provides Joshua with a real sense of confidence. He is perhaps remembering the crucial battle of the Israelites with the Amalekites on their way from Egypt to Canaan (Exodus 17:8ff) and the impressive figure of Moses high on the hillside, holding his hands up towards God to encourage the army. Joshua had been in the valley in the thickest of the fighting. It was Joshua who had borne the heat of the day and the responsibility of command. He would have been inspired by the confidence that Moses had in the Lord's promises.

Here he is in the same position, seeking to inspire the commanders under him. There is to be no question as to how the battle is going to turn out. He not only tells them that God will lead them to victory, in the symbol of the ark of the covenant he places him literally at the head of the army. The trumpets played by the priests represent the voice of God announcing victory, so they have the powerful voice of God. This all culminates in putting the voice of God into the mouths of his people, with their great shout, and the walls will tumble down.

Prayer

Let us pray that we fight God's battles and not our own. Amen

ROBG

17

Battle won

When the trumpets sounded, the people shouted, and at the sound of the trumpet, when the people gave a loud shout, the wall collapsed; so every man charged straight in, and they took the city. They devoted the city to the Lord and destroyed with the sword every living thing in it—men and women, young and old, cattle, sheep and donkeys.

God's total victory in bringing his people into the Promised Land is somewhat disturbing in its cruel finality. I can only explain it in terms of license to exaggerate. To include the destruction of donkeys, too, does suggest a further interpretation. It is written, perhaps, to assure the people of God's complete fulfilment of his promise. Though there is great acclaim for Joshua, the glory belongs to God alone. No battle could have been won unless all had been obedient to him.

I recently went into a shop where you can buy model armies. There were futuristic warriors from the year AD40,000 as well as traditional knights in shining armour. I was tempted to suggest a new set entitled Joshua's Army. The disturbing verse describing the destruction of every living thing (v. 21), suggests a possible war to end all wars. The people will come into a land of peace and security, with no hint of hostility or 'unrest'. It is a taste of what obedience to God will bring.

Many people reject the book of Joshua because they believe it is simply about warfare. Taken as a whole, however, the chapter emphasizes not so much warfare, but the power of God and his faithfulness to overcome. So often, God asks us simply to obey, even when it does not seem the most sensible or strategic thing to do. Sounding trumpets, whooping and shouting and marching round the city in itself do not offer much promise. The outcome, however, is not based on mere wishful thinking, raw emotion or clever manipulation. Instead, it is based on the signs that have been recognized throughout the pilgrimage from Egypt to the Promised Land, the signs given by God himself.

Reflection

'Peace I leave with you; my peace I give you. I do not give to you as the world gives. Do not let your hearts be troubled and do not be afraid' (John 14:27).

RobG

John 1—3

Each of the four Gospels has a different flavour. Mark is a man of few words, concise and quick—one of his favourite words is 'immediately'. Matthew is concerned with the Jewish world, showing how Jesus fulfils their expectations of the coming Messiah. Luke in his turn commends Jesus to the outsiders—the Gentiles—and, in doing so, commends him to all outsiders. I appreciate them all, but reading John feels like coming home.

The fourth Gospel is the most complex, with layers of meaning and repeated themes that make it perhaps more like a piece of music than most books. The writer misses out many of the stories from the other three Gospels, but they are replaced by profound meditations on a number of themes. Chapters one to three, which we will be reading for the next fortnight, see the first appearance of many of these themes—the cosmic sweep of God's work; Jesus as God's word; the gifts of life and light; the old order giving way to the new, and the Spirit as bringer of the new; God's love for the world and humanity that, at the same time, leaves us free to respond or not to respond; the profound interweaving of human and divine imaged in the word become flesh.

Who was the author of this very different Gospel? Tradition has it that this Gospel was written by 'the beloved disciple' who, in turn, has been identified as John, the son of Zebedee. This argument rests on a single text in the final chapter of the Gospel (21:20, 24). However, modern scholarship holds that this chapter is probably an appendix that was added later and, for that and other reasons, finds this authorship unlikely. Other possible authors are John the Elder, and John Mark, but it seems that it is impossible to be certain.

Lesslie Newbigin in *The Light Has Come* (Eerdmans, 1982) uses this very uncertainty to make a theological point, asserting that the author is deliberately and carefully hidden, so that we the readers will listen to the word, Jesus, to whom he witnesses, rather than to the author himself.

Whoever the author was, and whenever the Gospel was written (again there is no agreement on this), it is undoubtedly the fruit of long and deep meditation. It repays being read in the same way—slowly, with an eye and an ear for the themes and patterns that give it so much of its richness.

Helen Julian CSF

19

Long ago and far away

In the beginning was the Word, and the Word was with God, and the Word was God. He was in the beginning with God. All things came into being through him, and without him not one thing came into being. What has come into being in him was life, and the life was the light of all people. The light shines in the darkness, and the darkness did not overcome it. There was a man sent from God, whose name was John. He came as a witness to testify to the light, so that all might believe through him. He himself was not the light, but he came to testify to the light. The true light, which enlightens everyone, was coming into the world.

'In the beginning was the conversation.' This is how Erasmus, a great Reformation scholar, translated this opening of John's Gospel. It may seem too homely an image for such a passage—the great overture of the Gospel, introducing many of the themes that the evangelist builds on later. To use a more modern metaphor (reading this Gospel tends to set off a spate of metaphors), the first 18 verses are like the opening of an epic science fiction film—setting the scene, far back in time and far away in space. To use an ugly but useful word, it is like the prequel to an existing blockbuster.

However, then, into this cosmic sweep of a story comes 'a man'. He isn't accidental or anonymous. He was sent from God, and we know that his name was John. He had a purpose, too—to bear witness to the word, the life and the light that were there at the creation.

The human dimension has a place in this story and it is an essential place. God's word is not a monologue, but a conversation. From the beginning, there is dialogue between the divine and the human (see Genesis 1—3 for the first examples). At the opening of John's Gospel, we are on the brink of a new and more intimate dialogue.

Sunday reflection

Creator God, at the start of a new week, help me to remember my true beginnings in you and in your creating word. May our conversation this week be filled with your light and your life, that I may witness to others. Amen

HJ CSF

God with us

He was in the world, and the world came into being through him; yet the world did not know him. He came to what was his own, and his own people did not accept him. But to all who received him, who believed in his name, he gave power to become children of God, who were born, not of blood or of the will of the flesh or of the will of man, but of God. And the Word became flesh and lived among us, and we have seen his glory, the glory as of a father's only son, full of grace and truth.

John's first description of Jesus is as 'the Word', so perhaps it's appropriate that in John's Gospel there are several words with particular and complex resonances. 'World' is one of those, and verse 10 is easier to understand if we know what an ambivalent word it is for John. It can mean one of three things: the humanly created world or the whole created order or the 'lower' world in contrast to the world above. It is this latter 'world' that John says did not know the one who created the far greater 'world'—the whole of creation.

There is an enormous humility here. This is not a God who rides roughshod over his creation, but one who respects its separateness and gives it the choice of accepting and receiving or ignoring him.

Another rich word is the one translated as 'lived' in verse 14. Older translations often made it 'dwelt'. The original word has con-

notations of 'pitched his tent' or 'tabernacled'. Perhaps this last, though not a common word, is the best.

In the Old Testament, the tabernacle in the tent of meeting and then in the temple was the place where God's glory lived among his people (Exodus 33:7–11; 2 Chronicles 5:13–14). Now in the word made flesh—Jesus—God's glory is living in a new way among his people, and this way will not be temporary. God's glory eventually departed from the temple, but those who believe in Jesus become, by God's grace, children of God like him, and therefore also places where God's glory dwells.

Reflection

How can I show God's glory today to the world he both created and loves?

HJ CSF

Shock of the new

This is the testimony given by John when the Jews sent priests and Levites from Jerusalem to ask him, 'Who are you?' He confessed and did not deny it, but confessed, 'I am not the Messiah.' And they asked him, 'What then? Are you Elijah?' He said, 'I am not.' 'Are you the prophet?' He answered, 'No.' Then they said to him, 'Who are you? Let us have an answer for those who sent us. What do you say about yourself?' He said, 'I am the voice of one crying out in the wilderness, "Make straight the way of the Lord." ' as the prophet Isaiah said.

In this Gospel Jesus describes himself in the famous 'I am' sayings—the true vine, the good shepherd, the way, the truth and the life and so on. In contrast, John says 'I am not'. The religious experts try to fit him into their existing picture of how God has worked in the past and their expectation of how he will work in the future. If John is not the Messiah, perhaps he is Elijah, who was expected to come back as Messiah's herald?

John does not fit into their categories, but he does answer in a way that they should be able to hear, because it is rooted in the scripture, which is their only authority. Hearing is crucial because the only thing that John will say about himself is that he is a voice. He is a voice that does not speak his own words, but the words of the one who sent him. Jesus will say the same of himself to his disciples (John 14:10, 24).

John gives the religious experts their answer, but it is not about himself at all. He points them to God, to the God of their own history, who had led them through the wilderness and been with them in the tabernacle there. He points them to God who is not just history, but is still to come. The new thing that confounds their categories is rooted in what they already know, but they must abandon their expectations in order to see it.

Reflection

Am I able to hear the voice of God when it comes in ways, and says things, that do not meet my expectations?

HJ CSF

JOHN 1:25–27, 29–31 (NRSV)

The unknown Christ

They asked him, 'Why then are you baptizing if you are neither the Messiah, nor Elijah, nor the prophet?' John answered them, 'I baptize with water. Among you stands one whom you do not know, the one who is coming after me; I am not worthy to untie the thong of his sandal.' ... The next day he saw Jesus coming towards him and declared, 'Here is the Lamb of God who takes away the sin of the world!' This is he of whom I said, "After me comes a man who ranks ahead of me because he was before me." I myself did not know him; but I came baptizing with water for this reason, that he might be revealed to Israel.'

About himself John will say only what he is not. When Jesus walks into the picture, though, John makes a positive and very definite affirmation for the first time— 'Here is the Lamb of God'. The ability to do this is not, he insists, the result of human wisdom. He is in the position of the most menial slave who kneels at the feet of his master or a guest to untie their sandal straps. Just as Israel as a people has been chosen to receive the revelation of God, though it is a small and insignificant group of people, so John has been chosen to receive this new revelation. All that he does is intended to alert others to God's work.

This work is, in a sense, one of new creation. 'The next day' is one of a series of time references that mark out seven days from the day when John receives the deputation from Jerusalem to the wedding in Cana. God is creating a new people in the coming of Christ, and John's baptism is intended to prepare them, and us, to receive this much greater gift.

In the radical turning around of repentance, John's baptism in water may open their eyes to see who is already among them, though unknown and unrecognized. The creative word, God's first creation, has come to initiate the new creation—for those who have eyes to see.

Prayer

Gracious God, open my eyes to see you where you stand in my life and I don't see you. Teach me how to reveal you to my world. Amen

HJ CSF

Seeking, finding, seeking

The next day John again was standing with two of his disciples, and as he watched Jesus walk by, he exclaimed, 'Look, here is the Lamb of God!' The two disciples heard him say this, and they followed Jesus. When Jesus turned and saw them following, he said to them, 'What are you looking for?' They said to him, 'Rabbi' (which translated means Teacher), 'where are you staying?' He said to them, 'Come and see.' They came and saw where he was staying, and they remained with him that day. It was about four o'clock in the afternoon.

When a woman comes to join the Franciscans and is admitted as a postulant—the first stage in community membership—she is asked a simple question: 'What do you seek?' She replies, 'I have come to seek God and his will for me.'

Now it is obvious that she must in some sense have already found God, otherwise she would not be making this dramatic break with her previous life. It is also true, however, that God is always going on ahead and so needs to be sought today, and today, and today—each new day, in fact, God must be sought afresh.

John's disciples had made a commitment to him, but now God was moving them on. John helps them to do so, pointing out the way. Initially, they are not at all clear who they are following. 'Rabbi' is usually used in John by those who don't fully understand who Jesus is, so its use by the two disciples suggests that they are intrigued but not yet certain that this is really the Messiah.

Rather as newcomers to a Franciscan community learn whether or not this is their calling by coming and living with us, so the disciples respond to Jesus' simple invitation to 'come and see'. God must be experienced to be known; theoretical knowledge is not enough. God's creative word invites the two to his home to remain—or, to use a more resonant word, abide with him.

Seeking and finding spiral round each other, each new search leading to new discovery, which in turn sets off new seeking. Always, though, 'God's initiative precedes and evokes our search' (Lesslie Newbigin, *The Light Has Come*, Eerdmans, 1982).

Prayer

Gracious God, today and every day, I come to seek you. Amen

HJ CSF

God is in the details

On the third day there was a wedding in Cana of Galilee, and the mother of Jesus was there. Jesus and his disciples had also been invited to the wedding. When the wine gave out, the mother of Jesus said to him, 'They have no wine.' And Jesus said to her, 'Woman, what concern is that to you and to me? My hour has not yet come.' His mother said to the servants, 'Do whatever he tells you.' Now standing there were six stone water-jars for the Jewish rites of purification, each holding 20 or 30 gallons. Jesus said to them, 'Fill the jars with water.' And they filled them up to the brim.

It is the details in this story that add layers of meaning and resonance. 'On the third day' will immediately evoke the resurrection story for many. It also completes the 'week' of the new creation, as there are seven days from chapter 1, verse 19, to the wedding at Cana. The wedding marks the culmination, as the true bridegroom (see John 3:29) attends a Jewish wedding and transforms it.

Jesus does not come alone to the wedding, but with his disciples. Already they belong together; the new Israel, like the old, consists of God and people together. The wedding feast was an accepted symbol of the reign of God and the joy that it would bring. So, the true bridegroom, the Messiah, with his people, comes to celebrate at a human feast, which is tinged with the divine.

The rites of purification were intended to make people worthy to join in the party, but the detail of the six stone jars (one less than the perfect number of seven) that held the water hints that these old rites, though not wrong, would always be insufficient.

Finally, the wine runs out. The joy that we can create for ourselves, though real, in the end always fails. Mary's faith brings her to Jesus in the expectation that he can make good this shortfall. She is the model disciple, concerned for the details of human need, turning naturally to Jesus in that need and ready to respond actively to his reply.

Reflection

Am I open to the possibility of seeing God in the details of life and alert to the layers of meaning that they can open up?

HJ CSF

Signs of glory

He said to them, 'Now draw some out, and take it to the chief steward.' So they took it. When the steward tasted the water that had become wine, and did not know where it came from (though the servants who had drawn the water knew), the steward called the bridegroom and said to him, 'Everyone serves the good wine first, and then the inferior wine after the guests have become drunk. But you have kept the good wine until now.' Jesus did this, the first of his signs, in Cana of Galilee, and revealed his glory; and his disciples believed in him.

Wine, in Judaism, was a symbol of the Torah, the Law, the expression of God's will for his people. Here the water for purification, which could never entirely purify, is turned into new wine, the wine of the gospel, which fulfils and completes the Law. This wine comes in such quantities—at least 120 gallons—that it must have been a very memorable wedding! God gives with open hands and enormous generosity.

In giving, God uses human intermediaries—Mary and the servants. These are the people who know where the wine came from— not the bride and bridegroom or steward or guests, only Mary, the servants and disciples. The word translated 'servants' is the one used for 'deacons' elsewhere in the New Testament, so perhaps we are meant to identify the servants with the disciples—those who serve because they believe.

Their belief comes as a result of seeing the miracle, but equally important is understanding it. Jesus' signs in this Gospel invite belief but don't compel it. Elsewhere, miracles lead to rejection (11:45ff) or misunderstanding (6:14ff, 26). Some no doubt saw this miracle as simply a way of rescuing a host who had undercatered; others saw it as a sign of God's overflowing gifts of grace and so believed in Jesus, the revealer of God's glory.

Prayer

Generous God, open my eyes to see the signs of your glory, open my ears to hear your voice and do your will, open my life to your transforming power, that the new wine of your gospel may flow through me, to bring your joy to the world, and that all may believe in you. Amen

HJ CSF

JOHN 2:14–21 (NRSV, ABRIDGED)

True worship, true sacrifice

In the temple he [Jesus] found people selling cattle, sheep, and doves, and the money-changers seated at their tables. Making a whip of cords, he drove all of them out of the temple, both the sheep and the cattle. He also poured out the coins of the money-changers and overturned their tables. He told those who were selling the doves, 'Take these things out of here! Stop making my Father's house a marketplace!'... The Jews... said... 'What sign can you show us for doing this?' Jesus answered... 'Destroy this temple, and in three days I will raise it up.'... he was speaking of the temple of his body.

Just as at the wedding the true bridegroom came to the marriage feast, so now the true temple comes to the temple. Once again, the old and insufficient order is being replaced by what is new and more than simply sufficient in Christ.

His anger at the money-changers has been seen as a judgment on the commercialization of religion. It can be trivialized as a passage to be quoted by those against cathedral shops. However, there is a deeper meaning. One of the main functions of the money-changers was to ensure that the animals for sacrifice were not bought with Gentile coins. It was part of the concern for ritual and purity that had its roots in a genuine desire to serve the holy God appropriately, but it had become a way of drawing tight boundaries around the elect. Only those who could keep all the rules were fit to worship God.

By driving out the animals and the money-changers, Jesus makes the sacrifices of the temple impossible for a time. When asked to justify himself, Jesus refers obliquely to the impending end of sacrifice. Soon there will be no need for animal sacrifice, for God has provided the sacrifice that will end sacrifice (Genesis 22:8). The death and resurrection of Christ, the temple where God truly dwells, will bring to an end the Law and the worship at the temple and begin a new era of grace and worship 'in spirit and truth' (John 4:23).

Sunday reflection

Is my worshipping community a place of grace, inclusion and worship in spirit and truth? Are there rules and boundaries that keep people out of the Kingdom?

HJ CSF

One hand clapping

Now there was a Pharisee named Nicodemus, a leader of the Jews. He came to Jesus by night and said to him, 'Rabbi, we know that you are a teacher who has come from God; for no one can do these signs that you do apart from the presence of God.' Jesus answered him, 'Very truly, I tell you, no one can see the kingdom of God without being born from above.' Nicodemus said to him, 'How can anyone be born after having grown old? Can one enter a second time into the mother's womb and be born?' Jesus answered, 'Very truly, I tell you, no one can enter the kingdom of God without being born of water and Spirit. What is born of the flesh is flesh, and what is born of the Spirit is spirit.'

Nicodemus is a Greek name, and in this Pharisee's thinking there are both Jewish and Greek elements. His first words to Jesus are the sort of judgment that intelligent, discerning Judaism could make of Jesus, recognizing in him something of God's work.

You might expect that Jesus would encourage him, lead him on step by step to a deeper understanding, perhaps opening the scriptures as Philip did to the eunuch (Acts 8:26–35), so that he could step easily from his existing faith into this new faith. Jesus, though, is not normally that kind of teacher. His way of teaching is infinitely more daunting, more exciting, more challenging. It bears some likeness to the Zen Buddhist system of koans—apparently nonsensical statements, such as 'what is the sound of one hand clapping?'

The pupil in Zen uses the koan to break through their normal ways of thinking and come to enlightenment. Jesus puts to Nicodemus the apparent nonsense of being born for a second time as the only way into the Kingdom.

Perhaps he knew that Nicodemus would never be converted by intellectual argument and so took the conversation on to another plane, one where Nicodemus' usual intellectual skills were of no use. Sometimes God works through our strengths; sometimes he calls us to step out of them and be changed by embracing paradox and apparent nonsense.

Reflection
Am I willing to move beyond what seems to make sense in my search for God?

HJ CSF

Seeing through things

'Do not be astonished that I said to you, "You must be born from above." The wind blows where it chooses, and you hear the sound of it, but you do not know where it comes from or where it goes. So it is with everyone who is born of the Spirit.' Nicodemus said to him, 'How can these things be?' Jesus answered him, 'Are you a teacher of Israel, and yet you do not understand these things? Very truly, I tell you, we speak of what we know and testify to what we have seen; yet you do not receive our testimony. If I have told you about earthly things and you do not believe, how can you believe if I tell you about heavenly things?'

I was born in Edinburgh, which is a very windy city. Unlike the wind of the Spirit, it's usually very obvious where the Edinburgh wind comes from—straight from the North Pole!

The wind of the Spirit doesn't feature on the weather maps, but that makes it no less real. Nicodemus begins to be intrigued as Jesus speaks of this other reality—invisible, not under our control, but with the potential to change lives. His question, 'How can these things be?' is the question of an enquirer—'Can it happen to me?'

Once again, Jesus challenges and pushes him on. Nicodemus has seen some of the signs that have brought others to faith in Jesus as the Messiah, but he has not himself made that leap of faith. Jesus' actions are some of the earthly things—they happen in time, in the flesh, but their meaning does not end there. Properly understood, they contain a spiritual reality that points beyond themselves. John Marsh in his commentary on John (Penguin, 1968) uses physical birth as an example of an earthly thing, then goes on to describe heavenly things as events that have their real origin in God's actions, such as the birth of Jesus, God's Son.

The birth in the Spirit links together these two realities, as believers come to experience the world as the place where God has come and in which God works.

Prayer

Holy Spirit of God, blow me into the new world of the Kingdom, where earthly and heavenly things all speak of God. Amen

HJ CSF

The free gift

No one has ascended into heaven except the one who descended from heaven, the Son of Man. And just as Moses lifted up the serpent in the wilderness, so must the Son of Man be lifted up, that whoever believes in him may have eternal life. For God so loved the world that he gave his only Son, so that everyone who believes in him may not perish but may have eternal life. Indeed, God did not send the Son into the world to condemn the world, but in order that the world might be saved through him. Those who believe in him are not condemned; but those who do not believe are condemned already, because they have not believed in the name of the only Son of God.

'God so loved the world'—the text of a thousand wayside pulpits. It's hard to recover its first impact when it's been read and heard and preached on and perhaps meditated on many times. Reflection on it can easily tip over into an almost threatening 'look, this is how much God loves me, surely I must love him in return?' And the end of the passage can seem to support this unhelpful interpretation.

Perhaps looking at our own experience of giving and receiving gifts may help. The best present is one given purely for the joy of it—not because we hope the recipient will love us better or return the favour or be impressed by our generosity as real gifts have no strings attached.

This is how God gives. The gift is priceless—the ultimate costly gift of his own Son, himself. It is given out of pure love for the world, even though the world 'did not know him' (1:10). God gives, then waits humbly for our response. It is in the power of each of us to receive the gift of salvation given in the gift of his Son or reject it. God's fervent desire is that all will accept (3:17). However, true love gives freedom to the beloved. We are God's beloved, free to accept or reject the gift he holds out to us.

Prayer

How awesome is your respect for our freedom, God. Help us to use it well.
Amen

HJ CSF

Doing the truth

And this is the judgment, that the light has come into the world, and people loved darkness rather than light because their deeds were evil. For all who do evil hate the light and do not come to the light, so that their deeds may not be exposed. But those who do what is true come to the light, so that it may be clearly seen that their deeds have been done in God.

Another of the themes from the prologue makes its reappearance. Although the darkness cannot ultimately overcome the light that Jesus brought into the world, both darkness and light are still present and active. They are present and active in the world and within each person.

Just as the merciless light of the make-up mirror in a theatre dressing room shows up all the wrinkles and pores, so the light of Christ shows up the less lovely parts of ourselves. The temptation is to turn off the light or walk away.

Again, we are our own judges. We can always come into the light, but sometimes we prefer to stay in the shadows, where we don't have to see too clearly what we are doing, how we are turning away from God, hurting each other, refusing to care as we should for those in need. As Nicodemus had to move from the security of his intellectual knowledge into the seeming nonsense of faith, so moving from the darkness into the light means taking the risk of acting–of 'doing the truth'.

These are the deeds that Albert Schweitzer called 'acted prayers for the kingdom of God'. They are not done for our own gratification or glorification, but for the sake of the Kingdom. They are tokens of our allegiance to God.

Often it is hard to know what it is right to do. 'Doing the truth' and 'coming to the light' can be good touchstones. Does this action ring true with what I can see of God's will? Am I happy for this action to be seen and known by those around me and God? Does it spread light in the world or does it deepen the darkness?

Prayer

Dear God, help me to step today a little more into your light. Amen

HJ CSF

Brides of Christ?

Now a discussion about purification arose between John's disciples and a Jew. They came to John and said to him, 'Rabbi, the one who was with you across the Jordan, to whom you testified, here he is baptizing, and all are going to him.' John answered, 'No one can receive anything except what has been given from heaven. You yourselves are my witnesses that I said, "I am not the Messiah, but I have been sent ahead of him." He who has the bride is the bridegroom. The friend of the bridegroom, who stands and hears him, rejoices greatly at the bridegroom's voice. For this reason my joy has been fulfilled. He must increase, but I must decrease.'

I'm very thankful that I joined my community in the mid-1980s. It meant that I didn't have to dress as a bride when I became a novice, which had been the custom in many communities earlier in the century. Becoming a 'bride of Christ' wasn't something that drew me to the community.

That said, there is a place for this image, and it has profound meaning when applied not so much to the individual Christian but to the Church. Isaiah had looked forward to the coming of the bridegroom (Isaiah 62:5) and now John uses the image of a bridegroom and best man to point away from himself and towards Jesus. His disciples are perhaps trying to provoke him to indignation with their statement, but John does not rise to it. The best man does not covet the bride for himself, but rejoices that these two

people have found each other and love each other. There can be no rivalry between best man and bridegroom.

Perhaps there is a lesson here for our churches. In a competitive world, it's easy to try to rank our own church against others—we have more new members, they have better music, that one the best preachers. If people are coming to Jesus it's because they are being drawn by the Father and so success of a church (however it's measured) is not a human achievement but a gift of God. It should, therefore, not cause jealousy or despondency, but rejoicing.

Reflection

How might the images of the bride and the best man apply to me as an individual, and to my church?

HJ CSF

Trust and obey

The one who comes from above is above all; the one who is of the earth belongs to the earth and speaks about earthly things. The one who comes from heaven is above all. He testifies to what he has seen and heard, yet no one accepts his testimony. Whoever has accepted his testimony has certified this, that God is true. He whom God has sent speaks the words of God, for he gives the Spirit without measure. The Father loves the Son and has placed all things in his hands. Whoever believes in the Son has eternal life; whoever disobeys the Son will not see life, but must endure God's wrath.

At first sight, the contrast in the final verse is an odd one. We would normally expect the opposite of 'believe' to be 'disbelieve' or 'doubt', not disobey. However, the Greek word for 'disbelieve' also means 'disobey'. So, belief and disbelief are not just matters of intellectual agreement or dissent, but of acting on what is believed. They involve 'the setting and direction and persistence of a whole life' (John Marsh, *John*, Penguin, 1968). This passage sums up the dialogue between Jesus and Nicodemus, but the story is, frustratingly, unfinished. We don't know how Nicodemus responded to his searching conversation with Jesus. We don't know if he accepted Jesus' testimony and made a leap of faith into a new and bewildering world beyond what his mind alone could comprehend. We don't know if he accepted the gift of eternal life or turned away. We don't know which direction his life took.

However, we can know that the same dialogue and the same choices are open to us. God still sends his Son into the world, testifying to the truth about God. The Word still speaks the words of God and still offers the Spirit to those who will abandon themselves to its mysterious power. The 'obedience of faith' (Romans 16:26), to use a phrase of Paul's, whose feast many will celebrate today, still has the power to bring us to eternal life.

The light of Christ shone into the night of Nicodemus' questioning and still shines into our darkness, which cannot ultimately overcome it.

Prayer

God of life and light, bring me more deeply into the obedience of faith and the limitless life of the Spirit. Amen

HJ CSF

Jacob

The story of Jacob is one of those Old Testament epics of which most people have what might be called edited or muddled memories. 'Something to do with some soup and being hairy or not hairy or something? Doesn't he climb a ladder and wrestle with a bloke who turns out to be God? I seem to remember a bit about speckled goats or am I going completely mad?'

If these are the sorts of things that spring to your mind, don't worry because you are absolutely right, except that there are other things as well. There are two sisters—one beautiful and shapely, the other rather plain with some sort of eye condition. They both want Jacob and they both get him. Mind you, he gets both of them as well, which is perhaps not quite as wonderful as it might seem. There is the story of a callous rape and a truly excruciating, eye-watering revenge wreaked on the guilty party by the enraged brothers of the victim. There is an account of a strange, tumultuous night and a tale of deep, deep fear in the heart of a changed man—fear that the darkness of the past will blot out the light of possible reconciliation—and a burst of joy when that fear is not realized. Most important

of all, this is the story of God working hard to turn Jacob into Israel, a father of his people and the man after whom the chosen people of God were to be named.

So, where do we start? After being cheated out of his father's blessing by Jacob, Esau is planning to kill his brother in revenge. These readings begin at the point where Jacob has decided to leave home while he is still in one piece. His mother Rebekah has advised him to travel to Haran to seek refuge and a new home with Laban, her brother, and so Jacob leaves Beersheba.

Do also read the section indicated in brackets before reading the printed extract and the note. Get the full scope of the story and, above all, enjoy it.

Adrian Plass

Stairway to heaven

Jacob left Beersheba and set out for Haran. When he reached a certain place, he stopped for the night because the sun had set. Taking one of the stones there, he put it under his head and lay down to sleep. He had a dream in which he saw a stairway resting on the earth, with its top reaching to heaven, and the angels of God were ascending and descending on it. There above it stood the Lord, and he said: 'I am the Lord, the God of your father Abraham and the God of Isaac. I will give you and your descendants the land on which you are lying. Your descendants will be like the dust of the earth, and you will spread out to the west and to the east, to the north and to the south... I am with you and will watch over you wherever you go, and I will bring you back to this land. I will not leave you until I have done what I have promised you.'

Do you think Jacob really laid his head on a stone? Bearing in mind that they ate a lot of cheese in those days as well, it's not surprising that he had such extraordinary dreams!

I wish I could stop feeling so envious of these biblical characters who had such vivid and inspiring messages from God. I mean, this is real Warner Brothers stuff, isn't it? A stairway to heaven with angels processing grandly up and down as they conducted their business between earth and heaven. At the top, God himself waiting to offer the sleeping Jacob some mind-boggling promises. It certainly beats the kind of thing we tend to hear nowadays, doesn't it? 'I sort of have a feeling that the Lord might sort of be saying that maybe I ought to sort of do something or other, but I could easily be wrong.'

I suppose we must conclude that, in this or any other age, God will communicate whatever needs to be communicated in the best way possible. Having said that, it may well be that the low level of our expectations militates against the kinds of encounters with God that we read about here. I have a feeling in my gut (a theological expression) that my expectations are low in just about every area of the faith that means so much to me. I would love to be open to more.

Sunday reflection

Remove the veil, Lord. Amen

AP

GENESIS 28:16–22

Bethel

When Jacob awoke from his sleep, he thought, 'Surely the Lord is in this place, and I was not aware of it.' He was afraid and said, 'How awesome is this place! This is none other than the house of God; this is the gate of heaven.' Early the next morning Jacob took the stone he had placed under his head and set it up as a pillar and poured oil on top of it. He called that place Bethel, though the city used to be called Luz. Then Jacob made a vow, saying, 'If God will be with me and will watch over me on this journey I am taking and will give me food to eat and clothes to wear so that I return safely to my father's house, then the Lord will be my God and this stone that I have set up as a pillar will be God's house, and of all that you give me I will give you a tenth.'

Some years ago, in a book called *The Final Boundary* (Harper-Collins, 1990, 2000), I wrote a story about a snail called Bethel. At the time I had no idea what the word actually meant. I am intrigued to learn, on studying this passage, that it actually means 'House of God'—a fitting definition in the context of my story. I'm pleased. It's like something clicking into place.

Something certainly clicked into place for Jacob. God had promised him and his descendants a spectacular future and absolute security for as long as it took for those promises to be kept. I find Jacob's response interesting and a little amusing. He was impressed and awed by what had happened, but that didn't stop him from setting out the terms of the contract in a manner that can only be described as 'businesslike'. God's side of the bargain was to provide protection, food, clothing and an eventual safe return. If all these things were forthcoming, Jacob would accept the Lord as his God, undertake that the stone he had set up would be God's house and, practical to the last, would give back to God a tenth of everything that he was given.

This is not the evangelical way, is it? Or is it?

Reflection

It wouldn't do some of us any harm to set out clearly what we can do for God in return for what he has done for us.

AP

Thicker than water

While he was still talking with them, Rachel came with her father's sheep, for she was a shepherdess. When Jacob saw Rachel daughter of Laban, his mother's brother, and Laban's sheep, he went over and rolled the stone away from the mouth of the well and watered his uncle's sheep. Then Jacob kissed Rachel and began to weep aloud. He had told Rachel that he was a relative of her father and a son of Rebekah. So she ran and told her father. As soon as Laban heard the news about Jacob, his sister's son, he hurried to meet him. He embraced him and kissed him and brought him to his home, and there Jacob told him all these things. Then Laban said to him, 'You are my own flesh and blood.'

There is an occasional television series called *Surprise, Surprise!* The programme draws huge audiences, largely because it specializes in bringing together relatives who have not met for years and fear that they might never meet again. Mothers are suddenly confronted with long-lost sons. Brothers are reunited after a lifetime of separation. Grandmothers are able to cuddle the grandchildren that, until now, have been voices on the telephone or photographs in the post. I am always annoyed with myself for crying when I watch this programme because that is exactly what the programme-makers intend me to do. I'm just a softy.

When I read this passage, I find, again, that there are tears in my eyes about something that happened thousands of years ago to a man called Jacob. It isn't even as if Jacob has met cousin Rachel or Uncle Laban before. It must have been wonderful, though, mustn't it, after travelling so far, to discover people who were a part of him, linked by blood and by all the ties of family.

I have travelled quite a lot over the last couple of decades and I cannot begin to tell you what a difference it has made to meet up with members of my family in strange and perhaps slightly threatening places. I thank God for them, just as Jacob must have thanked God for Rachel and Laban at a time when his future looked uncertain, to say the least.

Prayer

Thank you so much that we belong to someone. Our hearts go out to those who don't. Amen

AP

The other woman

Jacob was in love with Rachel and said, 'I'll work for you seven years in return for your youngest daughter Rachel.' … So Jacob served seven years to get Rachel, but they seemed like only a few days to him because of his love for her. Then Jacob said to Laban, 'Give me my wife. My time is completed, and I want to lie with her.' So Laban brought together all the people of the place and gave a feast. But when evening came, he took his daughter Leah and gave her to Jacob, and Jacob lay with her. And Laban gave his servant girl Zilpah to his daughter as her maidservant. When morning came, there was Leah! So Jacob said to Laban, 'What is this you have done to me?'

If I could transport myself through time to this exact point in the history of Israel, I would take two presents for Jacob. The first would be a portable CD player (with plenty of batteries, for obvious reasons) and the other would be a Rolling Stones album that includes a track with enormous relevance to his situation. For several days, wives, workers, sheep and goats would hear nothing from the inside of Jacob's tent but the rasping petulance of Mick Jagger's voice singing, 'You can't always get what you wa-ant!'

A tinge of malice in my motivation? Yes. After all, he had it coming, didn't he? The conman had been soundly conned, so it is difficult to feel great sympathy for him. Apart from anything else, Jacob seems to have slept with Leah without any inkling at all that she was the wrong woman. This means, if we are to believe the contrast in the descriptions of the two girls, either that Jacob was so drunk after the feast that he was incapable of telling the difference or that he invested an absolute minimum of verbal and emotional communication in the consummation of his marriage. I suppose the seven-year wait might explain that.

What goes around comes around. Jacob would have understood that very modern saying. Perhaps he would have hung it above his bed to meditate on as he listened to Mick telling him what he already knew.

Reflection

You can't always get what you want, even if God is on your side.

AP

Marrying sisters!

When Rachel saw that she was not bearing Jacob any children, she became jealous of her sister. So she said to Jacob, 'Give me children, or I'll die!' Jacob became angry with her and said, 'Am I in the place of God, who has kept you from having children?' Then she said, 'Here is Bilhah, my maidservant. Sleep with her so that she can bear children for me and that through her I too can build a family.' So she gave him her servant Bilhah as a wife. Jacob slept with her, and she became pregnant and bore him a son. Then Rachel said, 'God has vindicated me; he has listened to my plea and given me a son.'

Friends of mine had two girls. The older girl was physically attractive, with a natural grace in her movements and the most beautiful dark eyes. The younger was plainer, but brighter and more tomboyish—a lively presence. I liked them both and I was amazed when their father said he couldn't wait to have at least one taken off his hands. 'But they're lovely girls,' I said, 'why would you want rid of them?'

'It's all right for you,' he said darkly. 'You don't live with them. They've shared a bedroom all their lives and they'll have to go on doing that right up to when the first one leaves home, *if* that ever happens, which I doubt! Their arguing and bickering and fights and borrowing each other's stuff and—and all the other things that happen are just about driving me round the bend.'

'Well, they're very nice when they're out', I said, trying to cheer him up a little.

'I'm afraid,' he said, 'that has ceased to be a comfort.'

My suffering friend should have written this bit about Rachel and Leah. He would have understood. What an extraordinary catalogue of conflicts and collisions is recorded here. Babies, servants, mandrakes, jealousy, anger. Being the father of two daughters can obviously be problematic, but marrying two forceful sisters—one beautiful and one plain—it doesn't bear thinking about.

Reflection

There never was some shining, biblical, ideal world. People are people, and ever more shall be so.

AP

Dirty work

'What shall I give you?' he [Laban] asked. 'Don't give me anything,' Jacob replied. 'But if you will do this one thing for me, I will go on tending your flocks and watching over them: Let me go through all your flocks today and remove from them every speckled or spotted sheep, every dark-coloured lamb and every spotted or speckled goat. They will be my wages. And my honesty will testify for me in the future, whenever you check on the wages you have paid me. Any goat in my possession that is not speckled or spotted, or any lamb that is not dark-coloured, will be considered stolen.' 'Agreed,' said Laban, 'Let it be as you have said.' That same day he removed all the male goats that were streaked or spotted, and all the speckled or spotted female goats (all that had white on them) and all the dark-coloured lambs, and he placed them in the care of his sons.

This Laban character makes Robert Maxwell look like an angel of light. What a twister!

You might remember a television series called *Minder*. The central character was called Arthur Daley. Arthur lived by buying items that were cheap and useless and selling them for as much as he could possibly get. His idea of satisfaction was to end each day with a pocket full of other people's money and the knowledge that he had given nothing to anyone. His promises were worthless. Occasionally, a victim of this chronic double-dealing would seek revenge. Usually Arthur avoided retribution by the skin of his teeth.

Jacob must have been tempted to seek revenge on his devious relative as soon as he realized that he had been cheated. In 14 years of hard work he had hugely increased the wealth of his uncle, but in terms of his own personal wealth, he had nothing. Fortunately, instead of letting his anger overwhelm him, he seems to have hung on to God's promises and, as we shall see tomorrow, albeit in a rather bizarre way, God did not let him down.

Prayer

Father, sometimes we rage at unfairness. Why should we put up with the bad things others do to us without seeking revenge? Help us to follow your agenda when these things happen and to leave the pursuit of justice to you. Amen

AP

He did what?

Jacob, however, took fresh-cut branches from poplar, almond and plane trees and made white stripes on them by peeling the bark and exposing the white inner wood of the branches. Then he placed the peeled branches in all the watering troughs, so that they would be directly in front of the flocks when they came to drink. When the flocks were in heat and came to drink, they mated in front of the branches. And they bore young that were streaked or speckled or spotted... Thus he made separate flocks for himself and did not put them with Laban's animals... In this way the man grew exceedingly prosperous and came to own large flocks, and maidservants and menservants, and camels and donkeys.

All right, let's just think about this. Let's assume for a moment that all of us who are reading, or are likely to read, this passage have an unshakeable belief in the unerring nature, infallibility and in-anything-else-you-like of scripture. Every detail is true down to the most obscure semi-colon in the most impenetrable section of the least accessible chapter of the most boringly technical book in the Bible. Even so, we must surely pause to critically examine the means by which it is claimed that Jacob managed to breed speckled and spotted sheep. His method? Simple. When the animals mated in front of striped lengths of wood, their offspring were correspondingly marked. Hmm.

I am reminded of a similarly cunning plan hatched by an impoverished local council down in the county of Gloucestershire. To prevent cows roaming from one area to another, they employed a man to paint stripes across the road so that the cows would be deceived into thinking a cattle grid had been installed. The sane among us will not be astonished to learn that the cows were cleverer than the council.

No, I don't believe in Jacob's breeding methods. What I do believe in is God's faithfulness. No doubt he had an embarrassed angel out with a divine paint pot and brush every night during the lambing season. Jacob got his speckled and spotted sheep, but only because the Creator was on his side.

Prayer
Thank you, Father, for topping up our silly ideas so that they work when they need to. Amen

AP

Time to go home

Then the Lord said to Jacob, 'Go back to the land of your fathers and to your relatives, and I will be with you.' So Jacob sent word to Rachel and Leah to come out to the fields where his flocks were. He said to them, 'I see that your father's attitude towards me is not what it was before, but the God of my father has been with me. You know that I've worked for your father with all my strength, yet your father has cheated me by changing my wages ten times. however, God has not allowed him to harm me.' … Then Jacob put his children and his wives on camels, and he drove all his livestock ahead of him, along with all the goods he had accumulated in Paddan Aram, to go to his father Isaac in the land of Canaan.

During a recent visit to America, someone spoke about the concept of 'terminating friendships'. Apparently it is fashionable in certain quarters to review one's relationships in order to establish whether or not they continue to be positive and productive. If you decide a particular friendship is going nowhere, you may wish to consider the option of informing your 'friend' (face-to-face with courage, by letter or e-mail without) that the relationship must end because it has ceased to be functional. This seems to me one of the worst and most potentially destructive ideas in the entire history of bad ideas, but, as is often the case with over-the-top notions, it does spring from a grain of truth. There are times, hopefully few and far between, when contact with another person may have become so negative, counterproductive or damaging to either or both that it is more helpful to break the connection than to attempt to mend it yet again.

That is what happened with Jacob and Laban. For different reasons, they had had enough of each other. Now was the right time to make the break. Add to this the fact that God had instructed Jacob in a dream to return home and there could be little doubt about what the right course of action was.

Sunday reflection

Father, the last thing we want is to make silly, hurtful decisions about ending relationships. If a friendship is not good for us, however, and we know you disapprove, give us the courage to act. Amen

AP

GENESIS 31:33–37 (NIV) (READ ALSO VV. 22–31, 38–42)

Laban's lost labours

So Laban went into Jacob's tent and into Leah's tent and into the tent of the two maidservants, but he found nothing. After he came out of Leah's tent, he entered Rachel's tent. Now Rachel had taken the household gods and put them inside her camel's saddle and was sitting on them. Laban searched through everything in the tent but found nothing. Rachel said to her father, 'Don't be angry, my Lord, that I cannot stand up in your presence; I'm having my period.' So he searched but could not find the household gods. Jacob was angry and took Laban to task. 'What is my crime?' he asked Laban. 'What sin have I committed that you hunt me down? Now that you have searched through all my goods, what have you found that belongs to your household?'

Some passages of scripture are so rich in life and detail, that our belief in the Bible as, among other things, a record of fact, is revived and refreshed.

Here is a graphic picture of Laban, certain he will find what he wants, but in a state of high tension because Jacob's God has warned him to watch his mouth (v. 24). Into his nephew's tent he goes, flinging stuff around as he hunts these personal 'gods' that he is convinced are hidden somewhere. Nothing! He turns the maidservants' dwelling upside-down, then Leah's and finally he rushes into Rachel's tent, only to find his youngest daughter sitting on her camel's saddle, complaining of period pains. The gods are nowhere to be found in this tent either. Baffled, Laban gives up.

Time for Jacob to get something off his chest at last.

'Come on!' he says, passionately righteous because he knows nothing of Rachel's theft and cunning, 'this stuff I've stolen—stick it out here and let's see what everyone thinks about it! Nothing? Right, well I've got one or two things to say to you, Uncle Laban. I've been with you for 20 years now. Your sheep...' and so on and so on. My questions are these: did Rachel tell Jacob the truth after Laban had gone and, if she did, what did he say?

Prayer

Thank you, Father, that, apart from everything else the Bible is and does, it can be very entertaining. Amen

AP

GENESIS 31:51–55 (NIV) (READ ALSO VV. 43–50)

Out of bounds

Laban also said to Jacob, 'Here is this heap, and here is this pillar I have set up between you and me. This heap is a witness, and this pillar is a witness, that I will not go past this heap to your side to harm you and that you will not go past this heap and pillar to my side to harm me. May the God of Abraham and the God of Nahor, the God of their father, judge between us.' So Jacob took an oath in the name of the Fear of his father Isaac. He offered a sacrifice there in the hill country and invited his relatives to a meal. After they had eaten they spent the night there. Early the next morning Laban kissed his grandchildren and his daughters and blessed them. Then he left and returned home.

This arrangement between Jacob and Laban transports me to childhood days when my two brothers and I argued over how much of the sitting-room floor each of us could reasonably claim for playing with toys. After 30 minutes or so of loud complaints and counter-complaints, my long-suffering mother would use anything handy to mark off three areas, threatening that anyone who strayed out of bounds would not play any more and—worst of punishments—his area would be divided between the others. This ensured peace for a while, but I recall my mother's regret that we couldn't settle our differences without barriers imposed by outside authority.

The compromise reached by Jacob and Laban was not ideal. Jacob had worked hard for crafty old Laban for years and had every right to all he had brought from Haran. There was no obligation to compromise. Laban, on the other hand, must have finally realized that he had squeezed all he was going to get out of Jacob. Perhaps he feared that with this powerful God on his nephew's side it would be safer to have Jacob safely and permanently on the other side of a witness heap. Still, they did part on good terms after a meal and Laban did get to kiss his daughters and grandchildren goodbye. A far better ending than might have been predicted.

Prayer

Father, may our differences be resolved in love rather than witness heaps. Amen

AP

Night wrestling

So Jacob was left alone, and a man wrestled with him until daybreak. When the man saw that he could not overpower him, he touched the socket of Jacob's hip so that his hip was wrenched as he wrestled with the man. Then the man said, 'Let me go, for it is daybreak.' But Jacob replied, 'I will not let you go unless you bless me.' The man asked him, 'What is your name?' 'Jacob', he answered. Then the man said, 'Your name will no longer be Jacob, but Israel, because you have struggled with God and with men and have overcome.' Jacob said, 'Please tell me your name.' But he replied, 'Why do you ask my name?' Then he blessed him there.

I feel I can identify with Jacob as I write this. I am suffering pain in my right hip—not because I have wrestled with God, but because I have arthritis. I expect the pain is about the same, though.

This bizarre experience of Jacob's happened at a crossroads in his life, the point where his dealings with Laban were over and he was full of dread about encountering his brother Esau the following day. It is not surprising that such a night should be filled with wrestling and conflict. I have known nights like that and so have many of you I'm sure, but what was going on here? It's all so strange. What can possibly be meant by the suggestion that Jacob was actually wrestling with God? Why was the man who turned out to be God unable to overpower a mere mortal? Why did God 'cheat' in the end by throwing out Jacob's hip?

Clearly it has something to do with the establishment of Jacob's new and more substantial identity as Israel, the father of a people—a man who has struggled with God and himself and survived. Perhaps the vigour with which Jacob fought and held on to the man/God was a significant measure of his determination to make the Lord's blessing his number one priority for the first time in his life. The touch on the hip was simply a reminder that, in the final analysis, the boss is the boss.

Reflection
Some of the best people bear the scars of God.

AP

45

Brotherly love

Jacob looked up and there was Esau, coming with his 400 men; so he divided the children among Leah, Rachel and the two maidservants. He put the maidservants and their children in front, Leah and her children next, and Rachel and Joseph in the rear. He himself went on ahead and bowed down to the ground seven times as he approached his brother. But Esau ran to meet Jacob and embraced him; he threw his arms around his neck and kissed him. And they wept. Then Esau looked up and saw the women and children. 'Who are these with you?' he asked. Jacob answered, 'They are the children God has graciously given your servant.'

'There are times when you get what you wa-ant!' This might have been Jacob's personal adaptation of Mick Jagger's song following the joy and relief of his restored relationship with Esau. After his endless, dream-filled, tumultuous night, his feverish, strategic dispersal of personnel and flocks and his general gut-wrenching dread of what the morning would bring, suddenly, amazingly, everything is all right, and the two brothers are almost competing over who can be the most generous.

Some years ago I 'brokered' a reconciliation between two Christians. One lady (let's call her Sally) had done something truly unspeakable to another (whom we'll call Vera). Sally wanted to sort this out, but lacked courage. She asked me if I would tell Vera what she had done and then be present at a meeting between the two of them. I shall never forget the encounter. It happened in the late evening in an old caravan at the end of our garden. Sally, terrified, and I, apprehensive, sat and waited in a silence that was broken only by the hissing of the old-fashioned gas lamps that lit the interior of the caravan. Then, the door opened, and in came Vera. The two women looked at each other for what seemed like several minutes but can't have been, then Vera took a step forward, opened her arms wide and embraced the person who had treated her so badly. It wasn't just a gesture—she meant it.

Prayer

Father, thank you that, when it is working as it should, the body of Christ is able to heal its own deepest wounds. Amen

AP

The unkindest cut of all

All the men who went out of the city gate agreed with Hamor and his son Shechem, and every male in the city was circumcised. Three days later, while all of them were still in pain, two of Jacob's sons, Simeon and Levi, Dinah's brothers, took their swords and attacked the unsuspecting city, killing every male. They put Hamor and his son Shechem to the sword and took Dinah from Shechem's house and left. The sons of Jacob came upon the dead bodies and looted the city where their sister had been defiled. They seized their flocks and herds and donkeys and everything else of theirs in the city and out in the fields. They carried off all their wealth and all their women and children, taking as plunder everything in the houses.

This passage makes my eyes water. I'm not talking about crying. I'm talking about imagination working far too well in identifying with someone else's pain. What a comprehensive revenge these brothers wreaked on Shechem and the other male Shechemites. I have no idea what would have been used to circumcise adult males at this point in history. I'm not sure I want to know. I have a nasty feeling that Simeon and Levi would have found a way of insisting that the implement in question must be blunt. Perhaps they claimed that horrible, unspiritual old sharpness would render the ceremony ineffectual. However, it was done. Three days later, the newly snipped Shechemites were still in so much pain that the attack by Dinah's brothers must have seemed nothing more than a whirling blur out of which swords

and spears emerged to end their pain and their lives.

Jacob seems to suffer something of a dip in his faith on learning what his sons have done. Despite God's earlier promises, he expresses a fear that, because of what has happened, he and his household will be attacked and destroyed by surrounding forces.

'You shouldn't have done that to Shechem', he complains. 'Well,' reply the sons, in the manner of all sons since time began who have gone their own way regardless of what anyone else thinks, 'he shouldn't have treated our sister like a prostitute.'

Reflection

Why is it that, at times, close family can seem so unspiritual and so right?

AP

Pure protection

Then God said to Jacob, 'Go up to Bethel and settle there, and build an altar there to God, who appeared to you when you were fleeing from your brother Esau.' So Jacob said to his household and to all who were with him, 'Get rid of the foreign gods you have with you, and purify yourselves and change your clothes. Then come, let us go up to Bethel, where I will build an altar to God, who answered me in the days of my distress and who has been with me wherever I have gone.' So they gave Jacob all the foreign gods they had and the rings in their ears, and Jacob buried them under the oak at Shechem. Then they set out, and the terror of God fell upon the towns all around them so that no one pursued them.

One of the interesting things about writing these notes is that often the message of the passage is specifically for me. If it happens to be for you also, well, that's wonderful. Here's a good example. Jacob has been told by God to go back to Bethel (where he used his stone pillow to build an altar, remember) and settle there. Jacob's response is a sort of frenzy of purification. False gods and anything else that God might not approve of are collected, bundled up together and buried under an oak tree at Shechem. Having done that he and his people are ready to march—a purified body acting in obedience to God's will. No wonder they seemed invincible to all those they passed.

I have something to do in obedience to God and I believe God is telling me through this part of Jacob's story that some purification is needed in my life before I take the next step in my personal odyssey. I'm not sure that I am completely happy about the obedience or the purification, but I do want to get things right. You may be facing the same kind of crucial challenges in your life. If so, let us pray together.

Prayer

Father, we are weak and flawed, but we want to be obedient. Show us the parts of our lives that are not clean and help us prepare to do what we are told. Amen

AP

Psalm 119

Anyone coming completely fresh to this psalm may well be puzzled by its peculiarities. With its 176 verses it is by far the longest in the Psalter, and the keenly observant will have noticed that it consists of 22 separate stanzas, each with 8 verses. The layout in the NRSV, with a single space between each stanza, doesn't make this obvious. The Good News Bible's layout, however, does. It gives each a sub-heading, as does the Eyre & Spottiswoode *Study Bible*, based on the RSV. In the Hebrew text, each stanza and every sentence begins with a letter of the Hebrew alphabet, following an A to Z order: Aleph, Beth, Ghimel… Resh, Shin, Tau. This is because Psalm 119 is what is technically known as an acrostic. You may well argue that such a method of presentation is distracting, but what we need to focus on is what the total psalm tells us about our dealings with God.

The message of these 22 stanzas has to do with the law of the Lord. The psalm deals with the value of that law, its provision of light and safety, its justice and the happiness to be found in it. The best of Israel's piety was exercised in offering unceasing gratitude to the lovingly kind God who so graciously bestowed upon his chosen people knowledge of his plan for right living. In response, they made it their foremost duty to live by that law and to discover in so doing the constant means of spiritual renewal and the glad fulfilment of their lives on earth.

The form the psalm takes may be a distraction, and no one seems to know why this acrostic form was used, but it has its fascination. Monsignor Ronald Knox, in his translation of the Bible from the Latin Vulgate, attempted to show the acrostic in English. The result is uneasy in places. His first stanza begins with A, and it runs 'Ah, blessed they, who pass through life's journey unstained…' In verses 129 and 131, which featured the letter R, Knox wrote: 'Right wonderful thy decrees are… Rises ever a sigh from my lips.'

The Old Testament scriptures contain other acrostic poems— Psalms 25, 34, 37, 111, 112 and 145, Proverbs 31:10–31, Lamentations 1–4 and, possibly, Nahum 1:2–8.

Colin Evans

What, never?

Happy are those whose way is blameless, who walk in the law of the Lord. Happy are those who keep his decrees, who seek him with their whole heart, who also do no wrong, but walk in his ways. You have commanded your precepts to be kept diligently. O that my ways may be steadfast in keeping your statutes! Then I shall not be put to shame, having my eyes fixed on all your commandments. I will praise you with an upright heart, when I learn your righteous ordinances. I will observe your statutes; do not utterly forsake me.

Who can be said to be 'blameless' or, as in another translation, 'faultless'? This 'alphabet of loyalty to the divine law', as Knox described Psalm 119, opens with an idealistic portrait of perfection. Can any of us, however conscientious we may be in our vows and pledges, be credited as doing no wrong? The Good News Bible translates verse 3 more emphatically, as 'they never do wrong'. Gilbert and Sullivan enthusiasts will recall Captain Corcoran, skipper of *HMS Pinafore*, who insisted confidently that he never swore at his crew, never used a 'big big D' and was never, never sick at sea! 'What, never?' they demanded cynically. 'Hardly ever,' he conceded penitently, when pressed.

We are all flawed creatures and, as Thomas Carlyle remarked, 'The greatest fault is to be conscious of none.' Paul stated 'that all have sinned and fall short of the glory of God'. The Jerusalem Bible freely and boldly renders this as 'both Jew and pagan sinned…' (Romans 3:23). It was nothing short of a miracle for a man like Paul, who had been among the most zealous adherents of the Law in Israel, to admit to being a sinner as a consequence of his confrontation with the risen Christ.

We find a humbler realism here in verses 5 to 8. The psalmist is so desperately keen to obey the divine decrees that he begs God to help him in so doing and never to disregard or forsake him. A suitable mood, surely, in which to go to church today.

Sunday reflection

In this world we cannot attain perfection, but we can step out on the right road, facing in the right direction.

CE

Does God punish us?

You have dealt well with your servant, O Lord, according to your word. Teach me good judgment and knowledge, for I believe in your commandments. Before I was humbled I went astray, but now I keep your word. You are good and do good; teach me your statutes. The arrogant smear me with lies, but with my whole heart I keep your precepts. Their hearts are fat and gross, but I delight in your law. It is good for me that I was humbled, so that I might learn your statutes. The law of your mouth is better to me than thousands of gold and silver pieces.

'God gives people trials,' said Muhammad Ali, stricken with Parkinson's disease. 'This is my trial. It's his way of keeping me humble.' Ali's belief that God punishes us may be part of his Islamic faith, but the stranger who asked to see me one evening long ago and held similar beliefs was a Christian. At one time he had been destined for the Roman Catholic priesthood.

He had once been a highly successful businessman with a large staff, but they had cheated and ruined him. He was sure, he told me, that the God who had, he believed, given him his material wealth had now deliberately dropped him in the gutter for particular moral lapses that he confessed to me. He painted a dark picture of God. I felt like quoting John Wesley who said to someone, 'Your God is my devil.' When the blows of life fall heavily on us, are we justified in regarding them as having been sent by God?

The psalmist portrays God as a stern teacher who resorts to punitive means to instruct him in the divine statutes and commandments. Hidden in the word for 'humbled' in verses 67 and 71 is the notion of chastening and punishment. The author of such verses here states that it did him good to be punished. It forced him to learn. To think of God only in this way, however, is to tread on dangerous ground. We may end up with a cruel God at odds with the revelation left to us by Jesus of a loving heavenly Father.

Reflection
The little boy had been told some of the Old Testament stories about God. Then he learned about Jesus, and he said, 'I love Jesus, but I hate God.'

CE

Any complaints?

My soul languishes for your salvation; I hope in your word. My eyes fail with watching for your promise; I ask, 'When will you comfort me?' For I have become like a wineskin in the smoke, yet I have not forgotten your statutes. How long must your servant endure? When will you judge those who persecute me? The arrogant have dug pitfalls for me; they flout your law. All your commandments are enduring; I am persecuted without cause; help me! They have almost made an end of me on earth; but I have not forsaken your precepts. In your steadfast love spare my life, so that I may keep the decrees of your mouth.

There is a tradition in Israel of grumbling at God. Elsewhere in the Psalms the supplicant shakes a fist heavenwards, complaining that the Lord has failed to come to his help in time of trouble (a typical example may be found in Psalm 44:23–26).

In the verses before us today, the suffering psalmist compares himself to a wineskin hung up indoors where smoke from the fire shrinks and blackens it. How long must he put up with the persecution heaped on him by his enemies? When, when, when will his prayers for help be answered? 'If God lived on earth,' goes an old Yiddish saying, 'people would knock out all his windows.'

We may disapprove of such improper sentiments expressed before God, yet there is a case for including some such in our rich treasury of Christian prayer. People in dire straits do feel forsaken by God, as Jesus did on the cross, and they need the opportunity to express their angry resentment against the Lord with suitably chosen words. In his 1,763 days of imprisonment in Beirut, Terry Waite, in his autobiography *Taken on Trust* (Coronet, 1994), tells of being desperate for signs of hope. He confesses that he got no comfort from his prayers, nor was the Bible of any use to him. Talking to himself he asked angrily, 'How dare you tell me to pray?' Isn't it to be expected that a realistic anthology of prayers is bound to include a liturgy of complaint?

Reflection

To be angry with God doesn't mean that we have stopped believing in him.

CE

Sweeter than honey

Oh, how I love your law! It is my meditation all day long. Your commandment makes me wiser than my enemies, for it is always with me. I have more understanding than all my teachers, for your decrees are my meditation. I understand more than the aged, for I keep your precepts. I hold back my feet from every evil way, in order to keep your word. I do not turn away from your ordinances, for you have taught me. How sweet are your words to my taste, sweeter than honey to my mouth! Through your precepts I get understanding; therefore I hate every false way.

Behind verse 103 lies an odd picture. We are taken into the classroom where young boys are trying to master their alphabet. The letters were written on a slate not with chalk but with a mixture of flour and honey. The pupils were told what each letter was and how it should sound. Then the teacher would point at random to a letter and ask the class which one it was and what it sounded like. The boy who was first to give the correct answer received a reward: he was invited to go up to the letter on the slate and lick it off. This sticky, messy custom was meant to be an incentive to learning.

If God's word is like honey, is it meant to be solely a soothing sedative? Some see their faith as a welcome escape from a hard, rough world to the sweet Jesus, and scripture can be quoted to support that view. On the other hand, in Ezekiel 2:8—3:4, the prophet receives his orders from God served up in the form of a written scroll that he is told to eat. Sweet as honey it was, but it contained a bitter, stinging message of lamentation and woe. In Revelation 10:10, John the Divine also receives a scroll that tastes like honey, but it upset his stomach.

The word of God to mankind stirs as well as soothes, disturbs more than it sedates.

Reflection

The hardness of God is kinder than the softness of men, and his compulsion is our liberation.

C.S. Lewis
CE

A time for hate

I hate the double-minded, but I love your law. You are my hiding-place and my shield; I hope in your word. Go away from me, you evildoers, that I may keep the commandments of my God. Uphold me according to your promise, that I may live, and let me not be put to shame in my hope. Hold me up, that I may be safe and have regard for your statutes continually. You spurn all who go astray from your statutes; for their cunning is in vain. All the wicked of the earth you count as dross; therefore I love your decrees. My flesh trembles for fear of you, and I am afraid of your judgments.

Our psalmist repeatedly tells us how he loves the law of the Lord. He also tells us that he hates the two-faced and every false way. Those who are uneasy about Christians, including any hatred of their credo, cannot escape the fact that elsewhere in scripture we are told that there is a time to hate as well as a time to love (Ecclesiastes 3:8). We are called to hate evil in its many forms. In our contemporary world, there is a lot of it about. From what we understand of the nature of God and his attitude to the human race, we may safely assume that he hates man's inhumanity to man just as much as we do.

Verse 119 paints a markedly vicious picture of God's hate. The writer likes to believe that the Lord treats the wicked 'like rubbish' (Good News Bible). The writer, we could say, desperately longs for God to smash their faces in. At verse 126 in the next stanza, the psalmist impatiently declares that 'it is time for the Lord to act'. In courtrooms, those who hate the accused have been known in their anguish to shout, 'I hope you get cancer' or 'I hope you rot in hell.' Such bitter hate may well make the gentle among us wince. Nevertheless, there is a time for hatred, but of deeds rather than of people.

Prayer

May it be thy will that no man foster hatred against us in his heart, that we foster no hatred in our hearts against any man.

The Talmud
CE

The insomniac

With my whole heart I cry; answer me, O Lord. I will keep your statutes. I cry to you; save me, that I may observe your decrees. I rise before dawn and cry for help; I put my hope in your words. My eyes are awake before each watch of the night, that I may meditate on your promise. In your steadfast love hear my voice; O Lord, in your justice preserve my life. Those who persecute me with evil purpose draw near; they are far from your law. Yet you are near, O Lord, and all your commandments are true. Long ago I learned from your decrees that you have established them for ever.

Insomnia is a common affliction that has many causes and it would be naïve to suppose that believers ought never to suffer from it! The misery of sleepless nights is a wretched experience. The poet Wordsworth was an insomniac and he dedicated three of his sonnets to sleep. As he lay in bed, the night hours passed till he heard 'the small birds' melodies' and 'the first cuckoo's melancholy cry'. He prayed that sleep, which had eluded him for three nights, would return on this, the fourth.

Whoever wrote Psalm 119, or at least the above portion of it, also seems to have been burdened with sleeplessness. He appears to be troubled by 'persecutors' and afflicted by what is now a medical condition known as paranoia. He feels as if he is surrounded, hemmed in by those hostile to him because he strives to keep the law of his Lord. Yet, he is sure of the divine presence and convinced of the truth of the statutes of God. Why then can't he sleep? The reasons may be merely mundane.

Perhaps his bed is uncomfortable or his bedroom is too warm or not warm enough. Maybe he ate too much too late. Possibly he is elderly and doesn't need so much sleep. Maybe it is worry about not being able to get to sleep that is the root of his problem, as he hears the clock strike every hour (verse 148) and restlessly he gets up before sunrise (verse 147).

Reflection

At least bear patiently,
if thou canst not joyfully.

Thomas à Kempis
CE

Deserving and disgusted

Look on my misery and rescue me, for I do not forget your law. Plead my cause and redeem me; give me life according to your promise. Salvation is far from the wicked, for they do not seek your statutes. Great is your mercy, O Lord; give me life according to your justice. Many are my persecutors and my adversaries, yet I do not swerve from your decrees. I look at the faithless with disgust, because they do not keep your commands. Consider how I love your precepts; preserve my life according to your steadfast love. The sum of your word is truth; and every one of your righteous ordinances endures for ever.

'I deserve to be saved,' says the psalmist, 'because I obey your law. I look down with disgust on those renegades who don't.' Here we get an early glimpse of the elder brother in the story of the prodigal son, a character with whom we tend to sympathize. Had he not stayed at home and worked hard for his father, while his younger brother had cleared off? Didn't he, rather than his brother, deserve the feast for services rendered, and the younger deserve an angry brush-off instead of a loving welcome?

The psalmist claims that he deserves divine favour because he sticks to the rules laid down by God's law. He also reserves the right to condemn those who refuse or fail to do so. Furthermore, he is sure the wicked will not be saved. How can he know? There are eternally significant matters about which even the totally committed believer is bound to be agnostic (meaning, not unbelieving but ignorant).

The revolution that Jesus brought with him from God puts love above law, the needs and the welfare of people beyond the meticulous observance of rules. He picked ears of corn in the fields for his hungry men on the sabbath, the day when work was forbidden by the Law. He referred to the time when David, to feed his own hungry men, even handed them the sacred bread from the house of God that only the priests were permitted to eat (Mark 2:23–28).

Reflection

Men of most renowned virtue have sometimes by transgressing most truly kept the law.

John Milton
CE

Seven times a day

Princes persecute me without cause, but my heart stands in awe of your words. I rejoice at your word like one who finds great spoil. I hate and abhor falsehood, but I love your law. Seven times a day I praise you for your righteous ordinances. Great peace have those who love your law; nothing can make them stumble. I hope for your salvation, O Lord, and I fulfil your commandments. My soul keeps your decrees; I love them exceedingly. I keep your precepts and decrees, for all my ways are before you.

Our psalmist often repeats himself. He keeps telling God how much he loves the Law and how well he has kept it. In fact, we might say he is full of self-congratulation! 'Consider how I love your precepts', he prays in verse 159. In the portion set for today, he reminds God, 'Seven times a day I thank you for your righteous ordinances.' An ancient rabbi, according to the Eyre & Spottiswoode *Study Bible* (see the footnote on p902), understood that God should be praised twice in the morning before reading the Ten Commandments and once after and twice in the evening before reading them and twice after. Those who pray today in our heavily secular culture would perhaps consider themselves to be doing pretty well to offer a short prayer first thing in the morning and another such at bedtime.

In the days of Jesus, the average person was expected to offer prayer at the time of the morning and evening sacrifices. The times of prayer were nine in the morning, noon, three in the afternoon and six. In the parable, we are introduced to the Pharisee as he congratulated himself on his moral and devotional life, counting it far superior to that of the penitent tax-collector standing nearby in the main inner quadrangle of the temple.

As we reach the end of these few studies of the longest psalm, we can take away with us the thought that we do well to strive for a disciplined devotional life, but without becoming too pleased with ourselves!

Sunday reflection

Let us pray in church today with the tax-collector in the temple—'God, be merciful to me, a sinner.'

CE

Two martyrs: Janani Luwum and Polycarp

For the next week, the readings will focus on two martyrs who are commemorated at this time of year—Janani Luwum and Polycarp. They come from opposite ends of Christian history, Polycarp having been killed for his faith in about 155, and Luwum as recently as 1977.

Janani Luwum was born in 1922 in Uganda and worked as a goatherd until he went to school. After training for the Anglican ministry in England, he became a bishop in 1969, and archbishop in 1974. By that time, the military dictator Idi Amin was in power. For a while, Archbishop Luwum was able to work with him. However, Amin became increasingly erratic and started to murder Christians and others whom he suspected of opposing what he was doing. Archbishop Luwum spoke out against the terror.

On 17 February 1977, Amin sent for the Archbishop. At one point, Luwum said, 'They are going to kill me. I am not afraid.' After that day, he was never seen again. Amin himself was overthrown the following year. Janani Luwum is commemorated in a statue on the west front of Westminster Abbey, which his widow and daughter came to see unveiled in 1998.

What we know about Polycarp (c.69–c.155) is less certain, but he was an important pivotal figure between the apostles themselves and the early Church. Like Janani Luwum, he was noted for his pastoral care as a bishop. He stood firm against heresies—particularly the Gnostics. He had been Bishop of Smyrna (in modern-day Turkey) for about 50 years when, in a random outbreak of violence, he was captured by a mob. They demanded his death and took him to the city's governor. The governor urged him to moderate his position as a Christian and show respect for Caesar. He refused and so was tried and killed. At his trial, he said that he had served Christ for 86 years and would not deny his master.

In the readings that follow, we shall look at the idea of being a martyr (which means 'witness') and how we are linked to them—even though their lives and sacrifices seem very different from anything we face.

I have drawn the Bible passages from *Exciting Holiness* (Canterbury Press, 1997) by Brother Tristam SSF. The book gives prayers and readings for lesser saints in the Church of England's calendar.

Rachel Boulding

2 TIMOTHY 4:1–2 (NRSV)

Seeing the world as God's kingdom

In the presence of God and of Christ Jesus, who is to judge the living and the dead, and in view of his appearing and his kingdom, I solemnly urge you: proclaim the message; be persistent whether the time is favourable or unfavourable; convince, rebuke, and encourage, with the utmost patience in teaching.

On this day 26 years ago, Janani Luwum was seen by his friends and fellow Christians for the last time. No one knows for sure how he was killed, but there's no doubt why this happened. He did exactly what is urged in this passage: he proclaimed the message in an unfavourable time. He convinced, rebuked and encouraged—not a worldlywise thing to do if the person you are rebuking is Idi Amin.

The reasons for this seeming recklessness are set out in the first few words: 'In the presence of God… and his kingdom'. In the presence of God, we need to raise our sights from the mundane and the terrifying and look to the widest possible picture we can imagine. This is a bit like those versions of our address that we've all written as children. They begin something like, 'Me, My bedroom, 22 Woodside Avenue' and end, 'Planet Earth, The Solar System, The Universe'. We need to order our priorities in terms of the eternal perspective of God's judgment of us all and of his Kingdom.

Even after fewer than 30 years, we can see that ruthless military dictatorships come and go. Janani Luwum realized this. Many Christians had been murdered before him during Amin's reign of terror and he knew the risks he was running. The regime was toppled the year after his murder.

Janani Luwum died for what was right and true and, in doing so, became a shining example to Christians in Uganda as they face their current trials, such as poverty and AIDS. How can we in the comfortable West follow his example? We can all raise our sights and see the world from God's perspective. Each one of us can 'convince, rebuke, encourage' (verse 2). I'm glad—and slightly relieved—that 'encourage' is in the list.

Prayer

Father, guide me in your ways so I can see the world as your Kingdom. Amen

RB

Just get on with it

As for you, always be sober, endure suffering, do the work of an evangelist, carry out your ministry fully. As for me, I am already being poured out as a libation, and the time of my departure has come. I have fought the good fight, I have finished the race, I have kept the faith. From now on there is reserved for me the crown of righteousness, which the Lord, the righteous judge, will give me on that day, and not only to me but also to all who have longed for his appearing.

This passage follows on from yesterday's reading. The writer suggests that his work and ours are all part of the same shared ministry, as if to say, 'Do your part; I've done mine.' He knows that any contribution, large or small, will be gratefully received.

I imagine this type of no-nonsense attitude might have appealed to Janani Luwum. He seems to have been one for getting on with the task in hand. When he was a bishop, he visited every parish in his large diocese. It was the same when he was an archbishop. With such a huge area to cover, he drove fast—although this did scare his clergy!

I wonder if, when facing certain death, he recalled this passage or similar ones. There is a warm sense of down-to-earth appraisal, of having done your best and then moving on. The writer doesn't boast about himself as being unique; he hands on the job and takes his place among the others 'who have longed for his appearing' (v. 8).

All this seems to hint at another thing the martyrs teach us. Much of our Christian life isn't about making a grand show of our Christian witness. It's about getting on with the jobs that we have been given. We all have opportunities each day to 'endure suffering, do the work of an evangelist, carry out ministry fully'. In the way we meet people, interact with family, friends, colleagues and strangers, we can all keep the faith.

Prayer

Heavenly Father, assist us with thy grace, that we may continue in that holy fellowship, and do all such good works as thou hast prepared for us to walk in.

From the General Thanksgiving, *Book of Common Prayer*

RB

My hope is in your judgments

O take not the word of truth utterly out of my mouth, for my hope is in your judgments. So shall I always keep your law; I shall keep it for ever and ever. I will walk at liberty, because I study your commandments. I will tell of your testimonies, even before kings, and will not be ashamed. My delight shall be in your commandments, which I have greatly loved. My hands will I lift up to your commandments, which I love, and I will meditate on your statutes.

Psalm 119, all through its 176 verses, keeps on about loving God's law and commandments. Sometimes it seems to protest too much so that it can appear to foster the sort of religiosity that is out of fashion at the moment, promoting an image of excessive, self-regarding and sentimental piety—too heavenly minded to be any earthly use. However, it's hard to imagine anyone really going too far in that direction, for anyone who loves God's law soon finds that it leads them not into smug navel-gazing, but outwards, to concern for others.

However, this balance between the inner life, alone with God, and outward actions, interacting with others, is something we have to negotiate afresh each day. As this passage implies, we can build sure foundations by meditating on God's statutes (as you are doing by reading this). In turn, this solid basis can give the confidence and the knowledge to be able to tell of your testimonies (v. 46).

So this passage suggests what lies behind any martyr's stance. The martyr is motivated by strong and steadfast love for God. We can all gain access to this love and draw on it, as martyrs do. What we can do now is prepare for those times of trial by meditating on God's commandments. Familiarity with God's commands (especially as they are set out in Psalms) will equip us for times of loss and grief, when we are feeling isolated and being let down by others. We might not literally tell of God's testimonies before kings, as Janani Luwum did before Idi Amin, but, holding on to that image of strength within us, we can face the tests that are part of everyday life.

Reflection

'In all thy ways acknowledge him, he shall direct thy paths'
(Proverbs 3:6, AV).

RB

Dying in order to live

'Very truly, I tell you, unless a grain of wheat falls into the earth and dies, it remains just a single grain; but if it dies, it bears much fruit. Those who love their life lose it, and those who hate their life in this world will keep it for eternal life. Whoever serves me must follow me, and where I am, there will my servant be also.'

'Good career move', a cynic said of Elvis Presley's death. We can all think of others who have died comparatively young and thereby seem to live on all the more strongly.

We keep hearing echoes of this idea of dying in order to live throughout the Gospels, but do we really live as if we believe it? Not often. We love our lives in a clingy way, as if we can't bear to be parted from our home comforts, financial security and reassuring possessions.

One of the difficulties with looking at martyrs is that there seems such an unbridgeable gulf between their lives of heroism and supreme sacrifice and our pathetic little offerings. We're not called to put our lives on the line, yet ordinary Christians are being killed in the world now—in Pakistan, Nigeria, Indonesia and Sudan, for example.

What we share with the martyrs is a life in Jesus as all our lives are hidden with Christ in God (Colossians 3:3). Suffering comes to us all eventually—perhaps in the form of bereavement or other losses (of health, relationships, status, job). We can see how whatever we go through, small or great, is taken up and shared by the God who suffers. He suffers on the cross and is with us in whatever pain we have to bear. So, in our own losses, we can try to trust God—not struggling on by our own efforts, but having faith in his power to change us. This is not to minimize the enormity of pain for those going through it, but to say that we don't go through anything alone.

What's more, the type of support for which we are grateful in our own troubles, great and small, is what we can give to others.

Reflection

'As you did it to one of the least of these who are members of my family, you did it to me'
(Matthew 25:40).

RB

Do not fear what you are about to suffer

And to the angel of the church in Smyrna write: These are the words of the first and last, who was dead and came to life: 'I know your affliction and your poverty, even though you are rich... Do not fear what you are about to suffer... Be faithful until death, and I will give you the crown of life. Let anyone who has an ear listen to what the Spirit is saying to the churches. Whoever conquers will not be harmed by the second death.'

If Janani Luwum's world of vicious dictatorships feels distant, although it's less than 30 years ago, that of Polycarp (c.69–c.155) seems even harder to grasp. Both, however, were killed by unjust rulers and there are still plenty of them today.

The book of Revelation was written some time late in the first century, within Polycarp's lifetime, but before he became Bishop of Smyrna in about 107. It's amazing that here is a text warning against persecution in a city where, some decades later, one of the major figures of the early Church faced just such persecution. These words would surely have been familiar to Polycarp. Did they inspire him as he faced the end: 'Do not fear what you are about to suffer... Be faithful until death'?

The 'second death' referred to here is the final punishment, at the judgment after death (Revelation 20:6, 14). John, the author, urges his readers and hearers to take a long-term view. This is, of course, something all martyrs have in common: they are prepared to risk everything because they realize that it's God's judgment that matters, not the casual brutalities of violent regimes. What seems to set them apart is this ability to look beyond immediate danger into infinity. Most of us would be much more wrapped up in our instincts of self-preservation.

Even though, thankfully, we are unlikely to be presented with such dramatic life-and-death choices, in our own way we do all have to make choices—whether or not to follow God. We're not likely to face death from an angry mob or a corrupt government because of our faith, but we do risk spiritual death if we ignore God's promptings.

Reflection

'Set your minds on things that are above, not on things that are on earth...' (Colossians 3:2).

RB

See your trouble as a well

I sought the Lord and he answered me, and delivered me from all my fears. Look upon him, and be radiant; and your faces shall not be ashamed. This poor soul cried, and the Lord heard me, and saved me from all my troubles. The angel of the Lord encamps around those who fear him, and delivers them. O taste and see that the Lord is gracious; blessed is the one who trusts in him. Fear the Lord, all you his holy ones, for those who fear him lack nothing.

In some ways, this seems an odd passage to choose for a martyr. To say that the Lord 'saved me from all my troubles' might, in common sense, suggest that the devout person was granted a pleasant life, full of blessings, rather than a violent death. It seems a strange way of witnessing to the idea that 'the Lord is gracious' and hears his people's prayers.

Of course, the psalm refers to a deeper sense of blessing. As with yesterday's passage, the setbacks of this transitory life are seen in perspective—a divine perspective that looks to the eternal rather than the temporal. This points us back to what we found in Thursday's reading: God doesn't promise an easy life.

Of course, it is how we meet this suffering that sorts the 'men from the boys'. Some people can take anything life throws at them and still 'see that the Lord is gracious' (v. 8). They are the ones who, as the Coverdale psalter puts it, 'going through the vale of misery, use it for a well' (Psalm 84:6, Book of Common Prayer). They use experience to learn more about themselves and to increase their sympathy for others. This doesn't mean that there is no pain, though—the process can take years.

Polycarp and other martyrs know their death is not in vain. It is not a random act of violence that proves how wicked the world is— no, it is a positive act of witness. The martyrs have stood up for their faith, paid the world's price, but have been blessed by God with ultimate rewards in a way the world cannot understand.

Prayer

Father, help me to see troubles as wells—positive chances for growth in love. Amen

RB

JOHN 15:1–5 (NRSV)

Do we fear the blessing of God?

'I am the true vine, and my Father is the vine-grower. He removes every branch in me that bears no fruit. Every branch that bears fruit he prunes to make it bear more fruit. You have already been cleansed by the word that I have spoken to you. Abide in me as I abide in you. Just as the branch cannot bear fruit by itself unless it abides in the vine, neither can you unless you abide in me. I am the vine, you are the branches.'

Today is the feast of St Polycarp, but we don't mark it specially this year as it falls on a Sunday. As Polycarp himself would have acknowledged, it's more important to celebrate Jesus' resurrection, which is what we are doing every Sunday.

Martyrdom must be the ultimate way of pruning in order to bear more fruit (v. 2). I don't mind nearly so much the sound of being 'cleansed by the word' (v. 3) and, still less, abiding in Christ (vv. 4 and 7)—those images have a much more comforting ring to them. Pruning, however, sounds painful as it implies that we have to lose something that might have been good. When you see pruned rose bushes, they look terrible, cut right down, almost dead.

This is an idea that makes us afraid of God, so that we push him away. If this suffering is what his love means, we don't want it, thank you. At the end of *Murder in the Cathedral*, T. S. Eliot's play

about the martyrdom of Thomas à Becket, the ordinary women of Canterbury say that they 'fear the blessing of God, the loneliness of the might of God, the surrender required, the deprivation inflicted'. We want to pass by on the other side and not get involved.

However, as we have seen throughout the past week's readings, you can't have one without the other. We can't go to church today, sing our hearts out and pray earnestly, then tomorrow avoid the Lord in the everyday business of life. No matter how lonely our suffering and, in the end, our death, God abides in us and we abide in him (v. 4). If we abide in God, we will be pruned, but we will also bear fruit.

Sunday reflection

Father, as we ponder the sacrifice of the martyrs, grant that we may see our sufferings in the light of theirs and turn to your glory. Amen

RB

John 4—6

John the Baptist had prepared the way for the coming of Christ. He had publicly testified that Jesus, on whom the Sprit of God had descended at his baptism, was indeed the Son of God. Jesus' own mission had now begun and he drew so many followers that the religious leaders began to watch him closely. The readings start as Jesus moves away from his critics in Judea and travels through Samaria, to have his provocative discussion with the woman at the well.

These chapters are full of miracles, healings and the teaching of a new theology. It was not easy. The healing of the paralysed man at the pool of Bethesda took place on a sabbath, which was construed by the Pharisees as breaking the Law and grounds for persecution. The miracles were great—5000 people fed till they could eat no more from five small barley loaves and two fishes. However, the people who witnessed it wanted to see more—'Do more miracles, and we will believe in you,' they said. This was not what Jesus came to do. His miracles were signs of his Father's glory, power and compassion. His mission was to bring eternal life to those who believed in him as the Son of God.

His claim to be the Son of God was tantamount to blasphemy to the religious leaders. Further, his teaching that people must feed on his body and drink his blood was the final straw to many who had followed him so far.

It is not easy for us today to accept all of Jesus' teachings or follow him with the whole-hearted commitment that he asks of us. For those who do, though, there are those springs of living water to draw from, the gifts of his body and blood to feed on and the scriptures of the Old and New Testaments to read in the light of the Holy Spirit.

The passages chosen here are not quite sequential for I have gone back through these chapters to include suitable readings for Ash Wednesday and the Women's World Day of Prayer. I like to think of these Christian women all over the world symbolizing the unity, love and reconciliation of the kingdom of God, heralded by John the Baptist and established on earth by Jesus, who we know as the Son of God, Saviour of the world and giver of eternal life.

Christine Chapman

JOHN 4:4–15 (NIV, ABRIDGED)

The gift of living water

Now he had to go through Samaria... Jacob's well was there, and Jesus, tired as he was from the journey, sat down by the well... When a Samaritan woman came to draw water, Jesus said to her, 'Will you give me a drink?'... The Samaritan woman said to him, 'You are a Jew and I am a Samaritan woman. How can you ask me for a drink?'... Jesus answered her, 'If you knew the gift of God and who it is that asks you for a drink, you would have asked him and he would have given you living water.' 'Sir,' the woman said, 'you have nothing to draw with and the well is deep. Where can you get this living water? ...' Jesus answered, 'Everyone who drinks this water will be thirsty again, but whoever drinks the water I give him will never thirst. Indeed, the water I give him will become in him a spring of water welling up to eternal life.' The woman said to him, 'Sir, give me this water so that I won't get thirsty and have to keep coming here to draw water.'

The people of Samaria were considered different, unorthodox in their faith and socially unacceptable to the Galileans and Judeans who were their neighbours on either side. The meeting between Jesus from Galilee and the woman from Samaria was not the most likely setting for a theological conversion. However, Jesus must have sensed that here was a woman who was unfulfilled and discontented with life, someone who needed just what he had to give, whether she recognized that or not. In fact, she seemed quite lacking in respect for him when he asked her for a drink.

Jesus was not put off. His own physical thirst was unimportant now as he saw his way to satisfying her spiritual thirst. Do you ever have a real spiritual thirst to experience the Spirit of God for yourself? Jesus showed himself as wanting to give the kind of water that only he could provide to an apparently undeserving and unappreciative person. Is there a sense in which we may identify with her and ask, 'Jesus, give me this water'?

Meditation

Take a few minutes to be still and focus on the spring of living water who is at the centre of your being.

CC

A hard nut to crack

He told her, 'Go, call your husband, and come back.' 'I have no husband', she replied. Jesus said to her, 'You are right... The fact is, you have had five husbands, and the man you now have is not your husband...' 'Sir,' the woman said, 'I can see that you are a prophet. Our fathers worshipped on this mountain, but you Jews claim that the place where we must worship is in Jerusalem.' Jesus declared, 'Believe me, woman, a time is coming when you will worship the Father neither on this mountain nor in Jerusalem... God is spirit, and his worshippers must worship in spirit and in truth.' The woman said, '...When he [the Messiah] comes, he will explain everything to us.' Then Jesus declared, 'I who speak to you am he.'

Jesus began his mission in Samaria with a difficult subject. He knew what the woman was like, yet he had God's love in him for her and he wanted her to know the true nature of God and his plan of salvation for the world. Only when he showed her that he could see straight through her did he succeed in cracking her hard shell. No sooner had she acknowledged that he must be a prophet of God, however, than she tried to distract him about the right place to worship—an issue about which the Jews and Samaritans had long disagreed. Jesus merely pointed out that it did not matter where people worshipped as God is spirit—he is not confined to a place—and what matters is that those who worship him are open to God in spirit. Presumably Jesus is speaking here of the Holy Spirit, whom he gives to all who believe in him.

The woman makes a last attempt to dismiss him by telling him that the Messiah will explain about these things, implying that he need not bother. Then Jesus reveals who he is—clearly, shockingly.

If we read on, we discover that by means of this unlikely, unreceptive woman of dubious moral standards, many people in Samaria came to a personal faith in Jesus Christ as Saviour.

Prayer

Jesus, if you bring people to me, give me your love and the right words to turn them to you. Amen

CC

JOHN 4:46–53 (NIV)

The faith of a non-believer

And there was a certain royal official whose son lay sick at Capernaum. When this man heard that Jesus had arrived in Galilee from Judea, he went to him and begged him to come and heal his son, who was close to death. 'Unless you people see miraculous signs and wonders,' Jesus told him, 'you will never believe.' The royal official said, 'Sir, come down before my child dies.' Jesus replied, 'You may go. Your son will live.' The man took Jesus at his word and departed. While he was still on the way, his servants met him with the news that his son was living. When he enquired as to the time when his son got better, they said to him, 'The fever left him yesterday at the seventh hour.' Then the father realized that this was the exact time at which Jesus had said to him, 'Your son will live.' So he and all his household believed.

This 'royal official' would almost certainly not have been a believer in God, but he had heard about Jesus' healing power and went to him in order to try to save his son's life. Jesus' critical response was probably directed more at the people around him than at this man, for Jesus did not want people to believe in him purely because of his miracles. He wanted them to believe in him for being himself, God's anointed one, who could save them from their sins and give them eternal life. However, he saw the man's faith and felt compassion for him. He healed the boy without even going to him. It also had the effect of bringing this influential man to belief in him that was based on more than his physical healing power.

There are times when we may find that we are asking God to devote himself to us and our needs rather than first devoting ourselves to worshipping him for who he is. Asking for God's blessings and help is fine—he gives freely in his compassion and love. However, God made us first to know, love and serve him. As we focus on this, our priorities and needs may change.

Prayer

Blessed are you, Lord our God, creator and redeemer of all; To you be glory and praise for ever.

Common Worship
CC

Where there is no faith

Now there is at Jerusalem... a pool,... having five porches. In these lay a great multitude of impotent folk... waiting for the moving of the water. For an angel went down at a certain season into the pool, and troubled the water: whosoever then first after the troubling of the water stepped in was made whole of whatsoever disease he had. And a certain man was there, which had an infirmity thirty and eight years. When Jesus saw him lie... he saith unto him, 'Wilt thou be made whole?' The impotent man answered him, 'Sir, I have no man, when the water is troubled, to put me into the pool: but while I am coming, another steppeth down before me.' Jesus saith unto him, 'Rise, take up thy bed, and walk.' And immediately the man was made whole, and took up his bed, and walked.

This reading is from the Authorised Version of the Bible because it contains a verse that is omitted from the other versions. It explains why the pool was believed to have healing powers and why you had to be a quick mover to be healed.

The disabled man appears very passive. When Jesus asks him if he wants to be healed, he just indicates that there is no point in even thinking about it as he has no one to help him. Someone else always gets there first.

Jesus cannot appeal to his faith, for the man has none. However, he does break through his apathy. There is a lot of energy in the order that has become so familiar to us—'Rise, take up thy bed, and walk.' Whatever it was that the man needed in order to be healed, Jesus gave.

Reading this encourages me to go on praying even when there seems to be no hope. We can surely bring people to Jesus in prayer and ask him to find a way of meeting them in their need. When we are discouraged and bemoan our own lack of support or impossible circumstances, maybe we need to get up and do something about it ourselves or pray that we may be shown a way through. This very thought may give us the energy we need.

Prayer

Jesus, grant me the gift of creative thinking—especially when I'm discouraged. Amen

CC

The gift of eternal life

'Very truly, I tell you, anyone who hears my word and believes him who sent me has eternal life, and does not come under judgment, but has passed from death to life. Very truly, I tell you, the hour is coming, and is now here, when the dead will hear the voice of the Son of God and those who hear will live. For just as the Father has life in himself, so he has granted the Son also to have life in himself; and he has given him authority to execute judgment, because he is the Son of Man.'

John's greatest concern in writing this Gospel was that those who read it might know for themselves a new quality of life given by Jesus to those who believe in him as God's Son. Most of us ask at some time what life is all about and, in particular, what our own life is about. The people of the Old Testament believed that life is a gift from God. One of Job's more constructive friends expresses this beautifully: 'The spirit of God has made me, and the breath of the Almighty gives me life' (Job 33:4).

In the passage above, Jesus is claiming that he, as God's Son, has the same power as his Father to give life. He calls it 'eternal life', which is there for all who believe that it was God who sent Jesus to his people on earth. He also claims that he, as God's Son, has been given the authority by his Father to judge God's people.

Eternal life, according to John, is life lived in loving fellowship with God, Jesus, the Holy Spirit and also those around us. The new life, which we experience from this fellowship, is experienced here and now and continues after our physical death in a fuller relationship with God and with Jesus. Those who are spiritually alive and come to know this kind of life will not be condemned at the time of judgment for they are in Christ.

Prayer

Loving Father, I believe that you sent your Son, Jesus Christ, to give us eternal life. Help me to acknowledge this, to claim it for myself, and to live in the power of the Holy Spirit. Amen

CC

JOHN 6:5–11 (NIV, ABRIDGED)

The faith of a child

When Jesus looked up and saw a great crowd coming towards him, he said to Philip, 'Where shall we buy bread for these people to eat?' He asked this only to test him, for he already had in mind what he was going to do. Philip answered him, 'Eight months' wages would not buy enough bread for each one to have a bite!' Another of his disciples, Andrew, Simon Peter's brother, spoke up, 'Here is a boy with five small barley loaves and two small fish, but how far will they go among so many?' Jesus said, 'Make the people sit down.'... Jesus then took the loaves, gave thanks, and distributed to those who were seated as much as they wanted. He did the same with the fish.

The feeding of the 5000 has become a household saying standing for the impossibility for us of feeding huge numbers without adequate provisions. It needed a miracle. John describes this, and all miracles, as 'signs' that point up a deeper truth.

Looking at the scene from the outside, we can see many truths emerging. Jesus cared about the physical needs of all these people. He wanted to provide for them and God gave him a way in which he could do that. Then he wanted the disciples to trust him, even though they could not see a way through the problem. They did—just. As for the crowds, he wanted them to expect something of him. They sat down and waited, but Jesus did not magically produce food from nowhere. It came from the crowd, in the form of five small loaves and two small fishes, offered in blind faith by one child. You can't tell me that no one else had any food with them on that day. It is this child, however, who offers the little he has and Jesus accepts it. He offers it to God and then starts to give it out, and give it out and keep giving it out.

On reading about this sign, can we see through to the deeper truth—that Jesus is the bread of life to us as we believe and trust in him and offer ourselves and all we have to him?

Prayer

Jesus, when I feel empty inside, help me to come to you first. Feed me with your life-giving Spirit. Fill me to overflowing. Amen

CC

We never know how he will come

When evening came, his disciples went down to the lake, where they got into a boat and set off across the lake for Capernaum. By now it was dark, and Jesus had not yet joined them. A strong wind was blowing and the waters grew rough. When they had rowed three or three and a half miles, they saw Jesus approaching the boat, walking on the water; and they were terrified. But he said to them, 'It is I; don't be afraid.' Then they were willing to take him into the boat, and immediately the boat reached the shore where they were heading.

Do you know that feeling when someone you love, who makes you feel fully yourself, suddenly leaves and you feel alone, a bit miserable and weak? Jesus had left everyone after the miracle of the feeding of the 5000 in which the disciples had been involved. The strength and the power that came from being with Jesus had gone. They set off back without him, though it was dark and windy and the waters were rough. Perhaps Peter, James and John did the rowing for they were used to it, with their heads down, pulling hard against the wind. The others may have been huddled up; some may have searched across the dark water for the land on the other side. They were about halfway when they thought they saw a figure coming towards them, apparently walking over the water. A ghost? They must have felt very exposed and vulnerable.

Then came the voice saying, 'It is I.' I do not think he meant, 'It's only me, Jesus.' I think he meant 'It is I, Son of God.' They welcomed him into the boat. Then, suddenly, they were there, having reached the shore again.

It is so important for us to be aware of Jesus' presence when we are low-spirited and feeling alone. We know he is there, but we may have to lift our eyes, look through our darkness and ask him to come into it. It may take some time—we never know how or when Jesus will come to us—but he always will.

Sunday reflection

Let us look for you, Lord, today, in our worship, in our fellowship, in those who need us. Amen

CC

'I am the bread of life'

So they asked him, 'What miraculous sign then will you give that we may see it and believe you? What will you do? Our forefathers ate the manna in the desert; as it is written: "He gave them bread from heaven to eat."' Jesus said to them, 'I tell you the truth, it is not Moses who has given you the bread from heaven, but it is my Father who gives you the true bread from heaven. For the bread of God is he who comes down from heaven and gives life to the world.' 'Sir,' they said, 'from now on give us this bread.' Then Jesus declared, 'I am the bread of life...'

Do you ever feel you have to do things, achieve, gain certificates and so on for others to recognize your worth? Just being you is not enough for some people. Yet, to those who know you well and love you, it is you they appreciate—not what you can do.

The people here are saying, 'Do something really miraculous—greater even than Moses did—and we will believe in you.' Moses had prayed to God to provide food for the Israelites in the desert and God had answered his request with the words, 'I will rain down bread from heaven for you' (Exodus 16:4). Manna had appeared for the people to make into bread. That was miraculous indeed, but Jesus put them right about who sent the bread from heaven. Not Moses, but God. He told them that God sends bread from heaven today. Then Jesus revealed himself as the bread of life, sent from heaven by God. This is the first of seven self-descriptions introduced by 'I am', identifying with God who revealed himself to Moses as 'I am', which is the inner meaning of *Yahweh*. Jesus was telling them that he, who was with them now, was the Son of God—divine, yet human, too.

Bread symbolizes a basic food. It is readily available, nutritious, satisfies our hunger, fills us. Let us be content to be ourselves, rather than striving to achieve, and become the people God created us to be by feeding on the bread of life, Jesus himself.

Prayer

Jesus, help me to look to you alone for my fulfilment in life. Amen

CC

Outrageous claims

'Whoever comes to me will never be hungry, and whoever believes in me will never be thirsty. But I said to you that you have seen me and yet do not believe... for I have come down from heaven, not to do my own will, but the will of him who sent me. And this is the will of him who sent me, that I should lose nothing of all that he has given me, but raise it up on the last day. This is indeed the will of my Father, that all who see the Son and believe in him may have eternal life; and I will raise them up on the last day.'

Jesus was making the most outrageous claims. Here was a man of known parentage, with no official position in the synagogue, speaking of his divine origin in heaven with God. He was telling the people that he had been sent to earth to carry out his Father's will, which was to give eternal life to those his Father gave him. Such talk was sheer blasphemy to the religious leaders, and he was certainly not the Messiah they had been taught to expect. No wonder they had difficulty believing him.

It is different for us. We have read the New Testament, which states that Jesus is the Son of God, who has the power to forgive sins, feed us with his life-giving Spirit, grant eternal life. It is different, but do we also have difficulty accepting these claims for ourselves? I still remember the moment when I felt weary of living with doubt and uncertainty and decided to give it a go. I prayed that Jesus would be real to me, that he would enable me to be truly repentant, that I might know the Holy Spirit in me. Nothing seemed to happen immediately, so I prayed again, and again. I think I really had to mean it. Slowly, almost imperceptibly, I found that I was praying to a real person, that I knew quite clearly what was not acceptable to God and recognized the very presence of God around and within me.

Prayer

Father, Son, Holy Spirit, may I know your presence—and respond in love.
Amen

CC

Discipline—with joy

'If I testify about myself, my testimony is not valid. There is another who testifies in my favour, and I know that his testimony about me is valid... I have testimony weightier than that of John. For the very work that the Father has given me to finish, and which I am doing, testifies that the Father has sent me. And the Father who sent me has himself testified concerning me... You diligently study the scriptures because you think that by them you possess eternal life. These are the scriptures that testify about me, yet you refuse to come to me to have life.'

Ash Wednesday begins the season of penitence, self-discipline, self-denial and singing the hymn 'Forty days and forty nights' in church to a rather mournful tune. I used to find it a bleak liturgical season at a bleak time of year. I even found it difficult to adjust suddenly to the joy of Easter. Now I try to start Lent with joy—the joy, and discipline, of making more time for prayer and stillness before God; the joy, and pain, of allowing the shadow side of my personality to surface before Christ; the joy, and sorrow, of deepening my knowledge of Jesus in his life and in his death.

In the passage above, Jesus is saying that it is his Father who reveals the true nature of his Son to those who are open to him. His Father sent him and gave him the power to work miracles and healings. His Father spoke through the prophets and in the scriptures, foretelling the coming of the Messiah. These people, though, think in human terms only; their minds are closed to the revelations of God.

It is God today who reveals Christ to us when we ask the Holy Spirit to guide our reading of the scriptures, to be in our relationships with other people, especially those with needs, to enter into our stillness and silence in prayer and to point to Christ in many other ways according to our individual personalities and gifts. May the 40 days and nights of Lent be a time of joyful openness, sound discipline and a real deepening of our relationship with Jesus.

Reflection

To become fully human we must surely be open to the divine.

CC

The body and blood of Jesus

So Jesus said to them, 'Very truly, I tell you, unless you eat the flesh of the Son of Man and drink his blood, you have no life in you. Those who eat my flesh and drink my blood have eternal life, and I will raise them up on the last day; for my flesh is true food, and my blood is true drink. Those who eat my flesh and drink my blood abide in me, and I in them. Just as the living Father sent me, and I live because of the Father, so whoever eats me will live because of me.'

Jesus now moves on from the concept of feeding on him as the bread of life to the more specific, almost cannibalistic concept of eating his flesh and drinking his blood. The people, including his disciples, could not help but recoil at the idea—as most of us would if we were not familiar with 'the body of Christ' and 'the blood of Christ' of our communion services.

Most Christian churches have made this eating of Christ's body and drinking of his blood a central part of their services using the symbols of bread and wine as at the Last Supper. However, Jesus was never one for outward rituals without real meaning behind them. The Quakers, who do not have sacraments or rituals, go straight for the inner meaning, or grace, behind the outward ritual. They receive Christ into themselves in the deep silence of their meetings for worship. To Jesus, it was vital that we receive him into ourselves. He must be part of us and we must be part of him as he is part of the Father. As we receive the bread and the wine, we may hear the words: 'Eat and drink in remembrance that he died for you, and feed on him in your hearts by faith with thanksgiving.' We receive Christ into our very being and may feed on him, drawing life from him, knowing ourselves to be forgiven and close to God through him, knowing his eternal life now and for ever.

Reflection
As part of your prayer life, try to be still for a few minutes each day, aware of Christ within you. Receive his love for you. Listen to him.

CC

77

Affirming women

Just then his disciples returned and were surprised to find him talking with a woman. But no one asked, 'What do you want?' or 'Why are you talking with her?' Then, leaving her water jar, the woman went back to the town and said to the people, 'Come, see a man who told me everything I ever did. Could this be the Christ?' They came out of the town and made their way towards him. So when the Samaritans came to him, they urged him to stay with them, and he stayed two days. And because of his words many more became believers.

Let us return today to the woman at the well in Samaria. The disciples expressed surprise at Jesus talking to her. It was not socially acceptable, though they did not like to say so. Now this woman was not backward in telling others. Her voice was heard and many others in Samaria came to believe in Jesus.

Many women throughout the world do not have this freedom to speak out or be heard or change their circumstances, and as global awareness increased in the 1950s so a sense of sisterhood between Christian women grew up, a sense of wanting to understand and share in others' concerns in prayer and love. So, the Women's World Day of Prayer was established for all Christian women of any denomination. Each year, a different country produces the service—it is always beautifully and sensitively presented—alive with symbols reflecting the culture of each country, shared by everyone.

Each year the service is concluded by everyone singing, 'The day thou gavest, Lord, is ended.' They sing of the sun rising in one part of the world as it sets in another, so the prayers and praises of the worldwide Church continue throughout one country's day and another's night. Women the world over are affirmed in their knowledge of being valued and loved by Jesus, and valued and supported by one another in prayer and love. Of such is the Kingdom of heaven—joined, of course, by our Christian brethren!

Reflection

'For we were all baptized by one Spirit into one body... If one part suffers, every part suffers with it; if one part is honoured, every part rejoices with it'
(1 Corinthians 12:13, 26).

CC

Backing off

When many of his disciples heard it, they said, 'This teaching is difficult; who can accept it?' But Jesus, being aware that his disciples were complaining about it, said to them... 'The words that I have spoken to you are spirit and life. But among you there are some who do not believe.' ... 'For this reason I have told you that no one can come to me unless it is granted by the Father.' Because of this many of his disciples turned back and no longer went about with him. So Jesus asked the Twelve, 'Do you also wish to go away?' Simon Peter answered him, 'Lord, to whom can we go? You have the words of eternal life. We have come to believe and know that you are the Holy One of God.'

Gone are the days when 5000 people would follow Jesus up into the hills, hoping to see another miracle or healing. Jesus was no longer saying what the people wanted to hear. He was saying unacceptable things about his divine origin and how they needed to eat and drink of him if they were to have eternal life. Understandably, from the human point of view, they backed off. Jesus did not soften his message to make it more acceptable as a result. He knew that God had prepared those with open hearts and minds to hear and receive him for who he was. As for the rest, he grieved for them, but they were not ready.

He did, however, feel the loss when so many of his followers drifted away. His question to his closest disciples, 'Are you going to leave me too?' sounds quite anxious. However, there is no hesitation in Peter's reply, 'We have come to believe, and know...'

There are many followers of Jesus today who back off when confronted with the warnings of Advent or the penitence of Lent, but who are quite happy to come to church at Christmas and Easter. However, if we really live in Christ and feed on him and allow him to live in us, then he will enable us to bear the whole of his teaching. He will also enable us to say, with Peter, 'We believe and know'.

Prayer

Father, open my heart to receive all of Jesus' teachings. Amen

CC

1 and 2 Thessalonians

Strategically placed on the Roman trunk road, the city of Thessalonica was a large centre of political, economic and religious life. As well as its settled urban population, it had a constant stream of traders and travellers, giving it a cosmopolitan flavour. To this city came the battle-scarred mission team of Paul, Silas and Timothy, full of evangelistic fervour, proclaiming the good news of Jesus Christ.

Paul, as was his custom, centred on the synagogue, arguing with the Jews on the grounds of scripture. Some of them were converted, as were many of the Greek adherents, and a number of the leading women in the city. Obviously this outraged the Jewish authorities and a mob set out to get rid of Paul and his companions. Unable to find them, they vented their anger on Paul's host, Jason, and took him and other Christian converts before the authorities, accusing them of entertaining those people 'who have been turning the world upside down' (Acts 17:6).

Jason was bound over to keep the peace, so Paul and his companions had to leave the city hurriedly—for their sake, Jason's and the church that had been established. It was not the end of the matter, though, for some of the mob pursued Paul and his friends to Beroea, causing them to have to move on yet again. They went to Athens and then Corinth. Read all about it in Acts 17 and you will see what a tough time it was, with a great deal of discouragement, disappointment and hardship.

Paul was desperate for news of the church in Thessalonica, so he sent Timothy back. Much to his joy and relief, Timothy returns with the news that the church is alive and well, in spite of persecution and internal problems. It is against this background that Paul writes to the church in Thessalonica, to praise and encourage them, refute allegations that have been made against him, address the subject of Christian living and explain what 'the coming of the Lord' means for them and, indeed, all Christian people. His second letter is very much a follow-up to the first, reaffirming the points he has made and addressing their anxieties.

What has all this to say to us in the Church of the 21st century? Let's find out together over the next two weeks.

Margaret Cundiff

1 THESSALONIANS 1:2–5 (NRSV)

Thanks be to God

We always give thanks to God for all of you and mention you in our prayers, constantly remembering before our God and Father your work of faith and labour of love and steadfastness of hope in our Lord Jesus Christ. For we know, brothers and sisters beloved by God, that he has chosen you, because our message of the gospel came to you not in word only, but also in power and in the Holy Spirit and with full conviction; just as you know what kind of people we proved to be among you for your sake.

Every Sunday when she came up to receive Holy Communion, Madge would say to me, 'Please pray for Terry Waite. I thank God for him, and pray for him every day.' Time went by, there was no word of Terry Waite, Madge grew frailer, then became housebound, so I took her Communion at home. Still she always made the same request: 'Please pray for Terry Waite. I thank God for him and pray for him every day.' Then came the wonderful day when Terry Waite was released from captivity. Madge was ecstatic, and tears of joy and thankfulness flowed as she said over and over again, 'Praise the Lord. My prayers have been answered.'

Our reading today reminds me of Madge, and others like her, as Paul speaks of his thankfulness and prayers for his fellow Christians in the city of Thessalonica, of the love and faith that sustained them day in, day out,

the bonds that held them together as brothers and sisters, 'beloved by God'. By our prayers we hold each other, support and comfort one another, bound together 'by cords that cannot be broken'—ever.

Today, thank God for the Church throughout the world and for the joy of being part of it. Remember those who are going through times of trial and difficulty, pray that they may be sustained and encouraged in their work and witness, and pray for yourself, that you may be constant in your remembrance of them, not just on Sundays but every day.

Sunday reflection

As o'er each continent and island, the dawn leads on another day, the voice of prayer is never silent, nor dies the strain of praise away.

John Ellerton (1826–93)

MC

Motivation and application

As you know and as God is our witness, we never came with words of flattery or with a pretext for greed; nor did we seek praise from mortals, whether from you or from others, though we might have made demands as apostles of Christ. But we were gentle among you, like a nurse tenderly caring for her own children. So deeply do we care for you that we are determined to share with you not only the gospel of God, but also our own selves, because you have become very dear to us.

Running through both of the letters to the church in Thessalonica is Paul's defence of his ministry and motives. Paul and his companions had been run out of town by bully boy tactics and so were unable to refute in person the slanderous statements that were being made about them. Paul appeals to the Christians through his letters to remember not just the message, and their manner in sharing it, but their way of life while they were living among them, giving everything they had and everything they were to enable that new life to be enjoyed to the full. 'Discredit the messenger and so destroy the message' is a well-known ploy, sadly often successful with the 'no smoke without fire' attitude many take on hearing gossip—hostile opinions and false accusations can sound so plausible.

It can happen to us in our own situation and we need to stand up and face the opposition, defend our cause—not out of our own pride and self-esteem, but for the sake of Christ whom we represent, whose name we bear. Equally, we must make sure that there is nothing in the way we present Christ or in our own personal lives that would cause others to doubt the authenticity of the news we proclaim. Paul could remind the church of how he came and how he behaved among them. Before God and before them, he is innocent of any charges. His public witness and private life are all of a piece. Is yours; is mine? How do we plead?

Prayer

Lord, fill me with your love that I may always reflect you in what I say, what I do and what I am, for your glory and for the Kingdom. Amen

MC

1 THESSALONIANS 2:11–13 (NRSV)

Training for the Kingdom

As you know, we dealt with each one of you like a father with his children, urging and encouraging you and pleading that you should lead a life worthy of God, who calls you into his own kingdom and glory. We also constantly give thanks to God for this, that when you received the word of God that you heard from us, you accepted it not as a human word, but as what it really is, God's word, which is also at work in you believers.

Yesterday we were reminded of Paul's 'mothering' of the new Thessalonian Christians. Today he speaks of his role as a father to them, overseeing their training and development, providing them with an example, urging them to fulfil their calling. He held constantly before them a vision of what lay in store, the inheritance that was theirs and they were pressing towards. They would need discipline of character, maturity to see through difficult and demanding situations and, above all, a clear concept of the life to which God had called them, and of his authority and power to sustain and enable them. They needed what we would call today an accelerated training scheme, a crash course in discipleship, each one of them given personal attention as individuals, in accordance with their own needs and abilities. Paul and his companions had to do that in a very short time while they were in Thessalonica. Was it enough?

This was not a matter of them simply following Paul's instructions, taking his word for it. They had received it through God's living word, Jesus Christ who had brought them into God's kingdom by what he had done for them. Now they could live as heirs of the kingdom of heaven with confidence, enabled by 'Christ in you, the hope of glory' (Colossians 1:27). In today's world, of which we are part and where we are called to work and witness, we have that same power within us, too, enabling us to live lives worthy of our calling, wherever we are, whatever our circumstance.

Reflection

'The mystery that has been hidden throughout the ages… but has now been revealed… Christ in you, the hope of glory' (Colossians 1:26–27).

MC

The pain and the passion

For you, brothers and sisters, became imitators of the churches of God in Christ Jesus that are in Judea, for you suffered the same things from your own compatriots as they did from the Jews, who killed both the Lord Jesus and the prophets, and drove us out; they displease God and oppose everyone by hindering us from speaking to the Gentiles so that they may be saved. Thus they have constantly been filling up the measure of their sins; but God's wrath has overtaken them at last.

As we read these verses, we can feel the sorrow and anger that Paul is feeling—he writes so strongly and fiercely about the way the Jews have been persecuting the Christians. Yet, he was once the chief of them—the memory of that must be so painful (see Acts 8:1–3). Now he is experiencing the same persecution from his fellow Jews, so he knows what it feels like, but, more than this, he knows it is how Jesus was treated, and the prophets before him.

Paul writes to the church in Thessalonica to assure them that they are not alone, that all Christ's followers are being attacked because his own people refuse to listen, refuse to accept him. Paul himself had been saved from the error of his ways (see Acts 9:1–31)—his eyes had been opened—but his fellow Jews had condemned themselves by their opposition to the truth. It is often said that converts to a cause are the most passionate. Perhaps this is because they realize what they were before and the full value of what they have discovered. Paul knows that he was once one of those who deserved God's wrath, but, by God's grace, he has been brought to not only know the truth, but also be empowered to share it.

To fully understand Paul's feelings on this matter, make time to read through Romans 9—11. His passion, pain and hope for his own people come through so powerfully and poignantly. Do we feel so strongly about our nearest and dearest who do not know Christ? How concerned are we about their eternal welfare?

Prayer

Lord, give me a passion for the truth, and the power to proclaim it.
Amen

MC

Glory and joy

As for us, brothers and sisters, when, for a short time, we were made orphans by being separated from you—in person, not in heart—we longed with great eagerness to see you face to face. For we wanted to come to you—certainly I, Paul, wanted to again and again—but Satan blocked our way. For what is our hope or joy or crown of boasting before our Lord Jesus at his coming? Is it not you? Yes, you are our glory and joy!

Paul felt so deeply for his fellow Christians in Thessalonica. After all, he and his companions had been the human agents who had brought them to faith. They experienced the joy of seeing more children born into God's family and delighted in their new brothers and sisters. The physical separation that resulted from persecution was like being torn apart in a war situation, the despair felt by bereaved families. Paul longed to see them again face to face, embrace them, look into their eyes, hear their voices, have the joy of reunion. Paul had 'a heart as big as a bucket' for his friends, those young converts, and he desperately wanted them to know he had done everything in his power to come to them again, but had been thwarted by Satan. Here he may have been meaning the hired mob that had chased them away, the authorities, those who had imposed a surety bond on Jason or circumstances that had held Paul, Silas and Timothy back. It is clear that all these forces were seen as agents of the devil to prevent God's work and purpose going forward, the Satanic power that sought to defeat and pervert God's grace.

Paul longed to see his Christian family again because he was so proud of them, but he looked forward even more to, one day, being in the presence of Jesus alongside them (v. 19). That would be the perfect fulfilment of his hopes and prayers, when he would finally see his ministry crowned by their faith, fortitude and service. What a wonderful family reunion that will be!

Prayer
Thank you Lord for the joy and blessings of being part of your family here on earth and in heaven. Amen

MC

To strengthen and encourage

Therefore when we could bear it no longer, we decided to be left alone in Athens; and we sent Timothy, our brother and co-worker for God in proclaiming the gospel of Christ, to strengthen and encourage you for the sake of your faith, so that no one would be shaken by these persecutions. Indeed, you yourselves know that this is what we are destined for. In fact, when we were with you, we told you beforehand that we were to suffer persecution; so it turned out, as you know… But Timothy has just now come to us from you, and has brought us the good news of your faith and love.

It was a tough decision to make. Timothy was the young, less experienced member of the mission team, but full of potential, a future leader. He had grown in leaps and bounds and was a vital partner. Paul wanted him by his side, but he was also desperate for news of the young church in Thessalonica and to give them support in their struggles. So Timothy is sent alone to visit Thessalonica—a dangerous mission that could cost him his life. He is not sent as an undercover agent, nor to issue instructions, but to strengthen and encourage the church. His job was to stand alongside them, be part of them, infuse them with comfort, courage and hope, bringing, by his presence, assurance of the power and presence of the Lord himself.

Waiting for news must have been a long and anxious time for Paul, but Timothy returns safely, bringing good news of the young church. Paul uses the Greek word *euangelizomai* when he writes 'good news'. It is the word he normally uses to describe the saving power of God in Christ—'the gospel'. This instance is the only other place where that particular word is used. Here it is a reminder of the faithfulness and love of God in Christ evidenced in his people. It is good news indeed and wonderful encouragement after a long, tough time—well worth waiting for!

Reflection

It is often at times of great stress and anxiety that the 'good news' comes afresh to encourage and cheer us. Look out for it today—and rejoice in it.

MC

Overflowing thanksgiving and praise

How can we thank God enough for you in return for all the joy that we feel before our God because of you? Night and day we pray most earnestly that we may see you face to face and restore whatever is lacking in your faith. Now may our God and Father himself and our Lord Jesus direct our way to you. And may the Lord make you increase and abound in love for one another and for all, just as we abound in love for you. And may he so strengthen your hearts in holiness that you may be blameless before our God and Father at the coming of our Lord Jesus Christ with all his saints.

The new church is in fine form, growing in faith, expressing love for God and for each other. Paul is proud of them all, and tells them so, but he doesn't give them a gold star and take them off his prayer list, feeling content that they can now go it alone. This is an ongoing process and he knows that there will be all kinds of setbacks, temptations, failures, and disappointments along the way. Paul assures them of his prayers, that they might be protected and encouraged, so that when the Lord returns they will be ready to meet him. Jesus is coming again and with him all those who have faithfully served him. Paul prays that the Thessalonian Christians will be fit to join them and a credit to the company of faith.

We need to ask ourselves if we have that same sense of urgency in our praying and whether or not that vision of the Lord's return inspires us to go on praying, loving and encouraging others in their faith and witness. It is so easy in our busy lives to allow our intercessions to become a lesser priority in the day. Paul led a busier and more hectic life than most of us can begin to imagine, but prayer was the central point of his ministry and pastoring, truly 'a labour of love'—may it be yours and mine also.

Reflection

How real to me is the promise of the Lord's return? What difference does it make to my prayer life and my work and witness today?

MC

1 THESSALONIANS 4:9–12 (NRSV)

Living it out

Now concerning love of the brothers and sisters, you do not need to have anyone write to you, for you yourselves have been taught by God to love one another; and indeed you do love all the brothers and sisters throughout Macedonia. But we urge you, beloved, to do so more and more, to aspire to live quietly, to mind your own affairs, and to work with your hands, as we directed you, so that you may behave properly towards outsiders and be dependent on no one.

Practical, spontaneous and often sacrificial love was the hallmark of the early Church. 'See how these Christians love one another' was the verdict passed on them, even by their enemies and opponents. The Christians in Thessalonica were a prime example. Their reputation had spread to many other parts, but Paul did not let them think that they had arrived. Instead, he urged them to continue and grow in love. He also directs them to some practical aspects of their lives that need some attention. A few of them are becoming a little restless, looking forward so much to the Lord's return that they are neglecting their personal responsibilities, so busy rushing around that they are failing to provide for themselves, relying instead on the goodwill of others. Paul nips that in the bud! (See also 5:12–22.)

So, then, how about you and me? How do we behave within our church fellowship? How does the world outside the four walls of our local church see us, I wonder? Do they say, 'See how these Christians love one another!' with admiration or with a sneer? What sort of a reputation have we got? As others meet us at work, in the supermarket, at the leisure centre, hear our conversations and see how we behave, what is their opinion not just of us, but also of the Christian faith that we profess? Maybe we need to examine our lives far more closely than we do and today, Sunday, is perhaps a good day to do it.

Sunday reflection

'If we say that we have no sin, we deceive ourselves, and the truth is not in us. If we confess our sins, he who is faithful and just will forgive us our sins and cleanse us from all unrighteousness' (1 John 1:8–9).

MC

1 Thessalonians 4:13–14, 17–18 (NRSV)

How will it happen?

But we do not want you to be uninformed, brothers and sisters, about those who have died, so that you may not grieve as others do who have no hope. For since we believe that Jesus died and rose again, even so, through Jesus, God will bring with him those who have died… Then we who are alive, who are left, will be caught up in the clouds together with them to meet the Lord in the air; and so we will be with the Lord for ever. Therefore encourage one another with these words.

Paul here gets down to the nitty-gritty of what is concerning the Christians in Thessalonica—namely, that they believe the Lord will return and take them to be with him, but what about those who have already died? What has happened to them? Will they miss out on the great day? Paul writes to assure them that those who have died in faith are already with the Lord and, when he comes again, he will bring them with him for the grand reunion. Then all will enter heaven together to be with the Lord for ever. What a picture, what a prospect!

After I have conducted a funeral, often someone will come up to me shyly and say, 'I know we will meet again one day, but where is he/she now?' My answer is always the same, 'With the Lord, absolutely safe!'

Paul's words are a great comfort and encouragement to me and are words that I share with others. We cannot cross all the 't's and dot all the 'i's, although one day we will. For now it is enough to rejoice in our glorious hope and look forward to the fulfilment of our salvation. As Jesus himself promised, 'Then the sign of the Son of Man will appear in heaven… And he will send out his angels with a loud trumpet call, and they will gather his elect from the four winds, from one end of heaven to the other' (Matthew 24:30–31). When will it be? We will think about that tomorrow!

Reflection

Nothing and no one can separate us from the love of God in Christ Jesus, our Lord. Read and rejoice in Romans 8:35–39 and share it with others.

MC

1 Thessalonians 5:1–2, 4–6 (NRSV)

When will it be?

Now concerning the times and the seasons, brothers and sisters, you do not need to have anything written to you. For you yourselves know very well that the day of the Lord will come like a thief in the night... But you, beloved, are not in darkness, for that day to surprise you like a thief; for you are all children of light and children of the day; we are not of the night or of darkness. So then, let us not fall asleep as others do, but let us keep awake and be sober.

Thieves often work under cover of darkness, the time when people are asleep or relaxing. Maybe a door is left unlocked, a window open, car keys lying around and then the thieves are in, out and away before we realize that they have been. Most of us have an 'it wouldn't happen to us' mentality, but it can and it does—so watch out!

Paul describes the coming of Christ as being like that—unexpected, quick and final. We need to live in a state of expectancy and readiness, like soldiers on red alert. Of course we should be getting on with everyday life, giving of our very best, eager to fulfil our calling, but knowing that at any moment our Lord, our Master, could return and we are ready to greet him. It is so easy to drift off, closing our eyes to the truth, in spite of all the reminders that we have been given. These reminders are not to frighten us to death, but to make us rejoice in the light and life of Christ and look forward to sharing in the great day of his return.

This season of Lent is a good time to shake ourselves up a little bit, get into training and make sure that we are fit to meet him, whenever and wherever he calls. As one of Charles Wesley's hymns encourages us, we should 'Rejoice in glorious hope, Jesus the judge shall come and take his servants up to their eternal home. We soon shall hear the archangel's voice, the trump of God shall sound, rejoice!'

For further reading, see Matthew chapters 24 and 25.

Prayer

Lord, may I be on active service, ready, waiting, working and rejoicing, for your coming again in glory. Amen

MC

Marching orders

And we urge you, beloved, to admonish the idlers, encourage the faint-hearted, help the weak, be patient with all of them. See that none of you repays evil for evil, but always seek to do good to one another and to all. Rejoice always, pray without ceasing, give thanks in all circumstances; for this is the will of God in Christ Jesus for you. Do not quench the Spirit. Do not despise the words of the prophets, but test everything; hold fast to what is good; abstain from every form of evil.

The instructions fly out, boom, boom, boom, in that staccato style that Paul often uses when he is anxious that nothing be left out. The directives are not just addressed to individuals, but to the whole company. For me it conjures up a picture of army recruits in training, being welded together as the instructor barks out orders. This is not just an endurance test, though—it is meant to be a pleasure, serving the King of Kings! 'Rejoice, pray, give thanks', says Paul. That surely is the secret of success: to be thankful and to enjoy the source of strength beyond human endeavour, allowing the Holy Spirit to direct and provide the incentive and power to succeed, being in constant communication with God by means of prayer.

Living the Christian life has never been easy—the history of the Christian Church shows that, but for us today it is still just as much of a battle. As Charlotte Elliott's well-known hymn puts it, 'Just as I am, though tossed about with many a conflict, many a doubt, fightings within and fears without, O Lamb of God I come!' Yet we rejoice and give thanks that 'The Lord is here, and his Spirit is with us', whatever the circumstances and wherever we find ourselves. As we attune ourselves to God in prayer, we will know for ourselves the joy of the Lord and being members of the greatest family of all time and for all eternity, both on earth and in heaven. So, heads up and quick march to the triumph song of heaven!

Reflection

Jesus says, 'So you have pain now; but I will see you again, and your hearts will rejoice, and no one will take your joy from you'
(John 16:22).

MC

2 THESSALONIANS 2:1–3, 5 (NRSV)

Get this straight!

As to the coming of our Lord Jesus Christ and our being gathered together to him, we beg you, brothers and sisters, not to be quickly shaken in mind or alarmed, either by spirit or by word or by letter, as though from us, to the effect that the day of the Lord is already here. Let no one deceive you in any way; for that day will not come unless the rebellion comes first and the lawless one is revealed, the one destined for destruction… Do you not remember that I told you these things when I was still with you?

The Thessalonians had been excited and delighted to hear from Paul, but some of them had got very hung up on what the Lord's second coming was all about. They had also been led astray by some people who had twisted Paul's words, cast doubts on his authority and, it would seem, also wrote letters pretending that they were from Paul. The church was in danger and so Paul writes a second time to them, warning them of what was happening, and spelling out yet again what he has already told them.

False messengers are still around today, appearing so genuine but causing havoc and they will continue to do so, which means that we need to be on our guard. Paul warns of a great final rebellion engineered by 'the lawless one'. Many will believe he is indeed God and will worship and obey him and be led to destruction. Those who have come before have been but pale imitations of him. He will be evil personified, a master of disguises, the power of darkness pretending to be the creator of light.

Terrifying thought, isn't it? We also need to be on our guard so that we are not led astray. Our strength lies in keeping close to God. As Peter writes in his first letter, 'Cast all your anxiety on him, because he cares for you. Discipline yourselves; keep alert. Like a roaring lion your adversary the devil prowls around, looking for someone to devour. Resist him, steadfast in your faith…' (1 Peter 5:7–9). This is the way to victory, whatever happens.

Prayer
Lord, keep me walking in the light of your love, that I may know the truth and follow it, all my days.
Amen

MC

Standing in the need of prayer

Finally, brothers and sisters, pray for us, so that the word of the Lord may spread rapidly and be glorified everywhere, just as it is among you, and that we may be rescued from wicked and evil people; for not all have faith. But the Lord is faithful; he will strengthen you and guard you from the evil one. And we have confidence in the Lord concerning you, that you are doing and will go on doing the things that we command.

Paul stops to take a breath, reflects on what he has been trying to convey to his Christian brothers and sisters and then asks them to pray for him and his companions. He needs their prayer support and he is not too proud to ask for it. He is very specific in his prayer request. First, he asks that the word of the Lord may spread and be received with joy and followed in obedience in all places, just as it had been in Thessalonica. Second, that he and his companions might be rescued from the dangers they find themselves in as they preach the gospel. Paul knows from bitter experience the opposition, the threats and the actual bodily harm he might constantly receive. He is realistic about his situation and the toll it takes on him mentally, physically and spiritually. Perhaps as Paul relates the needs, recognizes the battle that they are involved in, he loses his nerve for a second? If he does, he instantly regains it with the positive affirmation, 'But the Lord is faithful...' They pray in faith to their faithful God and Father, who provides the strength and the protection they need. Prayer unites them with the Lord and each other as brothers and sisters in the Lord, companions in the work of sharing the good news.

Never be too proud or independent to ask for prayer support from others. That is a special appeal to myself and to all ministers and leaders in the Church. May we all be constant in our prayer for one another, whether at home or away, always rejoicing in the faithfulness of God.

For further reading, see 2 Corinthians 11:22–28.

Reflection

Do I always keep my promise to pray for others? How faithful am I and how willing am I to ask for their support?

MC

Faith includes work

Now we command you, beloved, in the name of our Lord Jesus Christ, to keep away from believers who are living in idleness and not according to the tradition that they received from us. For you yourselves know how you ought to imitate us; we were not idle when we were with you... For we hear that some of you are living in idleness, mere busybodies, not doing any work... Do not regard them as enemies, but warn them as believers.

Paul's 'finally' of yesterday was not the end of the letter. There were problems that needed to be addressed and action recommended to them. He had already spoken about these things in his first letter (see Wednesday 19 March, 1 Thessalonians 5:14–22), but now he spells it out very specifically, for it would seem that the problem had got worse rather than better.

What was happening had all arisen as a result of misunderstandings about the Lord's return. Some believers had taken the view that, as the Lord would return any minute, what was the point of working, serving, sharing? They were happy to sponge off the others, while enjoying chatting, relaxing and generally being a nuisance and obstacle to others, both inside and outside the Church.

Paul brings down the full force of his disapproval on them. He reminds them that he and his companions worked for their living when with them, so that they would not be a burden to anyone and to set an example. The same went for all Christians, that if they didn't work, they didn't eat! This message was obviously addressed only to those who could work—not to those who were willing, but unable—and was advice to the Church as a whole as to their relationship with the offenders. Discipline and love go hand in hand and correction of error is necessary, both in the life of the individual and the work and witness of the Church.

So how should we view these disobedient, lazy believers in the church of Thessalonica and in our own churches today? They are not enemies—they are still our brothers and sisters. Warn them, discipline them, but never stop loving them. That's a fine balance, but, by God's grace, it can be achieved.

Prayer

The grace of the Lord Jesus Christ be with all of you. Amen

MC

Mary of Nazareth

For the next two weeks we have the privilege of glimpsing something of the life and character of Mary of Nazareth. Her 'yes' to God changed the course of history. Mary, a daughter of the Old Covenant (Luke 1:55), is the only person in the New Testament who is present at the opening of the Gospels, at the crucifixion and, finally, at the birthday of the Church. Spirit-filled, Mary is to be called 'blessed' for ever (Luke 1:48).

God's ways are not our ways (Isaiah 55:8). He delights in the unexpected—choosing this unmarried girl from Galilee, an area that was anything but kosher with its racial and religious mix of people. As Mary bears witness, God turns human values upside down. The powerful lose their place, the humble are lifted high, the hungry are filled, while the rich depart with nothing (Luke 1:52–53). When our feeble stores are exhausted, God uncorks the best wine and pours it out in great quantity (John 2:10).

Mary's trust in God is immense, yet even she experiences doubt and sorrow. Mary has to 'let go and let God', not just once, when, knowing the cost, she accepts God's will, but many times. She learns the discipline of blessing and the secret of joy. Her heart is pierced—the old man, Simeon, had prophesied this, singing of peace as he held her child (Luke 2:29, 35). Her journey, like ours, leads to the foot of the cross where her son will point her towards a new faith-family to help her grow towards Easter and Pentecost. We need the family of faith, too, as we journey through crucifixion, resurrection and renewal. Mary carried the life of Christ in her and this is our task, too. 'God's plan is to make known his secret to his people, this rich and glorious secret which he has for all peoples' (Colossians 1:27, GNB). And what is this secret? Staggeringly, it is 'Christ in you, the hope of glory' (v. 27, AV).

As we walk with Mary, we shall learn that seeming defeat turns to triumph because the distorted body broken on the cross, our ultimate hope and the crux of our faith, is the authentic expression of love.

Jenny Robertson

You are good enough for God

For thus says the high and exalted one who lives eternally and whose name is holy, 'I live in the holy heights but I am with the contrite and humble, to revive the spirit of the humble, to revive the heart of the contrite.' ... 'But my eyes are drawn to the person of humbled and contrite spirit, who trembles at my word.'

Mary said, 'You see before you the Lord's servant, let it happen to me as you have said.'

In recent months in Warsaw, I have been teaching PSE—personal and social education. Among other things, we cover aspects of self-esteem. One girl couldn't think of anything positive to write about herself. In the end, we decided that she was a good listener.

Ideas of fostering our self-esteem are very modern and would even surprise young people in other cultures in our own day, too. Mary of Nazareth, who would have been no older than the girl I taught, confidently asserted that 'all generations will call me blessed' (Luke 1:48). This, though, is because she knows for sure that 'the Almighty has done great things for me' (v. 49). Although, as we shall see on Tuesday, Mary freely questions the angel, she is afraid and trembles at God's word (Luke 1:29, 34).

God does not choose Mary because of her position in society or her education (she probably had no formal schooling), but her faith in his promised salvation is so strong that she allows God to take over her life completely. Mary is young and inexperienced, but her trust in God is total. She agrees to bring the Messiah to birth. Her simple consent changed the whole course of history. So, never say you are not good enough—you are good enough for God.

Others—known and unknown to her—also wait for God to save his people. Elizabeth, Zechariah, Joseph, the shepherds, Simeon and Anna, the crowd gathered in the Temple to whom aged Anna bears witness—all hope against hope for deliverance to dawn. Their humble, hidden lives count for God. Like Mary, they are all special people God is waiting to use for his glory.

Sunday reflection

There is no limit to what God will do through us if we trust him enough.

Archbishop William Temple

JR

The love-song of the Lord

I will leave in your midst a meek and humble people, and they shall trust in the name of the Lord... Sing, O daughter of Zion! Shout, O Israel! Be glad and rejoice with all your heart, O daughter of Jerusalem! ... The Lord your God in your midst, the mighty one, will save; he will rejoice over you with gladness, he will quiet you with his love, he will rejoice over you with singing.

In his short book, Zephaniah, a contemporary of Jeremiah, foretold disaster, judgment—and joyful restoration. Mary belongs to those 'meek and humble people' whose trust is so great that the Lord fulfils his purposes quietly, but with might and power and tremendous joy.

Meekness, humility, hiddenness have little value in our publicity-conscious age. Self-promotion, image, self-sufficiency are what count, but the daughter of Zion is commanded to rejoice because God loves her so much that he sings for joy! Early Church theologians concluded that Mary is the new 'daughter of Zion', but, in fact, Mary knows she is one of many daughters, an heiress to all the covenant promises of God. Mary's walk of obedience will take her to the cross. There, in the heart of seeming darkness, the Lord quiets her with his love (John 19:25–27).

Like the daughter of Zion, Mary rejoices because God has done great things for her (Luke 1:49). She has discovered that the secret of joy lies in the power of praise. The Lord rejoices over those who rejoice in him. A friend of mine keeps a thank you book. She wrote, 'The way to make room for grace is to receive more grace. Thank you, Lord!' Gratitude makes us glad and this makes God glad, too! This is the love song of the Lord. Let us listen for this love song. Perhaps we only hear the traffic outside, someone else's television, children's voices, our own emptiness and wandering thoughts caught up in so many agendas, but the prophecy of Zephaniah, fulfilled in the witness of Mary and other trusting, hidden people in the opening pages of the Gospel, assures us that we are part of the love song, too.

Prayer
The Lord rejoices over me and sings. Let me be quiet in that love. Amen

JR

Changing the course of history

The angel Gabriel was sent by God... to... Mary... The angel said to her, 'Rejoice, highly favoured one, the Lord is with you; blessed are you among women!' But... she was troubled at his saying, and considered what manner of greeting this was. Then the angel said to her, 'Do not be afraid, Mary, for you have found favour with God. And behold, you will conceive... and bring forth a son, and shall call his name Jesus.'

In Luke's Gospel, important events often occur away from the public eye. Mary's meeting with the angel, which changed the course of history, took place at home (Luke 1: 26–38). Western Christians express 'the lowliness of his handmaiden' by depicting Mary busy with domestic chores in a humble home. The Eastern Orthodox Church, following traditions from the 2nd century, teaches that Mary, educated in the Temple and fed spiritually with heavenly bread until she brought the Bread of Life into the world, was engrossed in contemplative study of Isaiah 7:14: 'Behold, the virgin shall conceive and bear a Son and shall call His name Immanuel.' Icons show her weaving with red thread, a symbol of the salvation that came from the life that she was to bring into the world.

People in Mary's time mostly lived in large households, but we usually imagine Mary alone when the angel arrives (vv. 26, 28). When Gabriel (meaning 'God is Mighty') first appears in scripture, the sight is so awesome that Daniel's strength ebbs away and the men with him flee, terrified (Daniel 10:7). Zechariah was struck dumb when he questioned Gabriel (Luke 1:18–22), but the angel patiently allows Mary to show her perplexity and ask, 'How can this be?' (v. 34). Our false self-regard or poor feelings about ourselves make us impose conditions on God's acceptance of us. We are often unable to face the deepest truths about ourselves, but Mary has the courage of great simplicity and trust. She takes God at his word, no matter what the consequences will be. The choice is hers and she gives unqualified consent.

Reflection

The angel's visit takes the covenant of the Old Testament into the pages of the New and into our lives and prayer. There is no compulsion, only love freely offered and unhesitatingly given. Let it be!

JR

The joyful discipline of blessing

Mary... entered the house of Zacharias and greeted Elizabeth. And... the babe leapt in her womb; and Elizabeth was filled with the Holy Spirit... and said, 'Blessed are you among women, and blessed is the fruit of your womb! But why is this granted to me, that the mother of my Lord should come to me? For indeed, as soon as... your greeting sounded in my ears, the babe leaped in my womb for joy.'

A friend, called to a war-torn country, writes, 'I need a lot of prayers in this work.' God calls, but never leaves us unsupported. The angel has told Mary about a soul-friend who could share her delight (v. 36), so she visits her relative, Elizabeth.

The meeting between these two women, both expecting their first child, is one of the most moving encounters in scripture. The intimate domestic setting is vibrant with faith, joy and blessing. The Holy Spirit has overshadowed Mary; the Son of God has begun to live within her. Elizabeth's unborn baby, who will prepare the way for the Lord, leaps in his mother's womb for joy. Elizabeth, filled with the Holy Spirit, blesses Mary with the authority of an anointed prophet.

Elizabeth's pregnancy, late in her life, can't have been easy. She must have felt very conspicuous, the butt of gossip, sharing her dumb husband's frustration at his God-given punishment because he had failed to believe the very thing her pregnancy witnesses. If Mary needed Elizabeth's counsel and advice, Elizabeth needed Mary's friendship and trust. It can take a lot of faith to acknowledge the hidden potential in one another, but Elizabeth unreservedly acknowledges unmarried Mary as 'the mother of my Lord'—a clear statement that the child to be born of her is none other than the Holy One of God.

Elizabeth blesses Mary twice and her unborn child once (vv. 42, 45). We are often too reserved to show our feelings, but, when we bless one another, we grow in love. Instead of trying to change the other person, we give them permission to be. Blessing is powerful. It brings growth and more blessing. It releases creativity and joyful praise —and Mary's Magnificat will be our reading tomorrow.

Reflection
Practise the joyful discipline of blessing.

JR

Holy is his name

'My soul magnifies the Lord... all generations will call me blessed. For he who is mighty has done great things for me, and holy is his name... He has put down the mighty from their thrones, and exalted the lowly. He has filled the hungry with good things, and the rich he has sent away empty. He has helped his servant Israel, in remembrance of his mercy... to Abraham and to his seed for ever.'

Mary's hymn of praise, still part of our worship today, might well have been sung in the earliest days of the Church's life, but it looks back to the Old Testament, too. It echoes three Old Testament praise poems by women. The first, by Mary's namesake, Miriam, sister of Moses, as she led the women in a triumphant dance, magnifies the Lord who 'has triumphed gloriously' (Exodus 15:21). The song of Deborah, one of the earliest poems in the Bible, challenges political leaders—'Hear, O kings! Give ear, O princes' (Judges 5:1–31)—but, like Mary's Magnificat, it is also concerned with justice and the poor. Mary's song, though, most closely echoes Hannah's thanksgiving for Samuel's birth: 'The Lord makes poor and makes rich; he brings low and lifts up. He raises the poor from the dust and lifts the beggar from the ash heap, to set them among princes and make them inherit the throne of glory' (1 Samuel 2:7–8). The song reminds us that God's promises are 'to Abraham and his seed for ever'. Could Mary's testimony as daughter of the covenant be the basis for discussion between Jews, Christians and Muslims?

Mary prophesies that the hungry will be fed, the rich go away empty; the mighty shall be put down, the humble lifted high. In the Beatitudes, Jesus teaches the paradox of power made perfect in weakness—that the humble, the despised, the empty, the broken-hearted, all are blessed (Matthew 5:3–10).

The heart of Mary's song will become the focus of her son's whole life—'holy is his name'. It is said that these words are the essence of religion and redirect our lives as we submit our plans, our money and our dearest dreams to God's holy will.

Reflection
Hallow God's name, desire God's will and trust God's power.

JR

Layers and depths

And she brought forth her first-born son, and wrapped him in swad-dling cloths, and laid him in a manger, because there was no room for them in the inn... And they [the shepherds] came with haste and found Mary and Joseph, and the babe lying in a manger. Now when they had seen him, they made widely known the saying which was told them concerning this child... Mary kept all these things and pondered them in her heart.

C.S. Lewis described heaven as being like an onion—you peel one layer off only to reveal another. The same is true of the Nativity. Was the birth in a cave in the hills as Eastern Orthodox icons show or a tumbledown stable as in Western art? Was there an inn or was it some relative's house, so overcrowded with visitors that Mary had to give birth among the animals in the lower room and bed the baby in the feeding trough? Do the words 'first-born' imply that Mary had other children? What about the manger? Significantly, Luke refers to it twice and commentators note the link with Isaiah 1:3, a reproach to Israel that became represented in Christian art. How are we to understand it now?

Layers of debate and yet the wonder of the whole event never ceases to make an impact. God comes to us in the simplest way imaginable, so that the youngest child in a Nativity play understands what's going on. In coming as a newborn baby, God hallows every birth. The babe of Bethlehem opens great depths to the meaning of mercy.

The shepherds gossip the good news and people marvel, but, says Luke, 'Mary kept all these things and pondered them in her heart.' We expect quick answers. Mary is patient and wise. She knows how to think deeply. She will need this ability as she follows her son through his public ministry into Pentecost. As mentioned in the introduction to these readings, Mary is the only person in the New Testament who is present at the beginning of the Gospels, at the crucifixion and at the birth of the Church.

Reflection

An obituary describing a musician said he was modest, yet incredibly deep, talented and so unassuming you'd never guess he was a star. Does this fit with Luke's picture of Mary? What have we learnt from her so far?

JR

The strange blessing of sorrow

Now, Master, you are letting your servant go in peace... for my eyes have seen the salvation which you have made ready in the sight of the nations; a light of revelation for the Gentiles and glory for your people Israel... He is destined for the fall and for the rise of many in Israel... and a sword will pierce your soul too—so that the secret thoughts of many may be laid bare.

Luke's birth stories began in the temple with Zechariah burning incense before the altar. Now we are back in the temple again. Joseph and Mary come to fulfil the Law and the Holy Spirit prompts Simeon to come in at exactly the right moment. Simeon blesses the seven-week-old baby and pours out praise. The parents are surprised (v. 33), but it is another confirmation of the truth of the angel's words, 'that the holy one who is to be born will be called the Son of God' (Luke 1:35, NKJV) However, when Simeon blesses Mary, he promises her sorrow (2:35).

God's love makes us whole, but pain is in the story from beginning to end. An elderly Christian friend calls this the mystery of mysteries. He wrote to me, 'I keep returning to the deepest affirmation of St John's Gospel: the Passion is the revelation of the Glory—not something that has to be gone through in order to get at a subsequent glory.'

Mary rejoiced at the touch of God in her life, but she also had to learn to bear the strange blessing of sorrow. The sword of sorrow mentioned in Zechariah 12:10 and Ezekiel 14:17 is destined for the Messiah and for Israel, too—another deep mystery. In post-Holocaust Poland railway sidings, a deserted worship-place, a grave-yard empty of stones, Hebrew inscriptions revealed as post-war paintwork fades, take on poignant significance. They are scant remains of a thousand years of Jewish life that were wiped out in the space of three years. A rabbi in war-ravaged Warsaw wrote that, although the sorrows of Israel were as deep as the sea and as high as the heavens, God weeps with his people with grief so great that the angels hide their faces.

Reflection
I am afraid of the sword of sorrow, but the Lord bears it for me.

JR

Infinite wisdom and love

When he was 12 years old, they went up for the feast as usual... Jesus stayed behind in Jerusalem... Three days later, they found him in the Temple, sitting among the teachers, listening... and asking them questions... and his mother said... 'My child, why have you done this to us?...' He replied, '...Did you not know that I must be in my Father's house?' But they did not understand what he meant.

Mothering Sunday has so many lovely associations. We think of spring flowers, chocolates and cards and children saying 'thank you' to their mums. Mothering Sunday came about when young people in domestic service were given an annual day off before Easter. On their way home, they picked wild flowers for their mothers who had ten kids and no washing machines. Fast food was unknown and the family was sacrosanct. Any deviation was punished and dealt with in secrecy or by outright rejection. Nowadays, as marriages fail, 50 per cent of children lose contact with their birth father just a couple of years after divorce. Few families attend church, but we are more open about failure, more welcoming to those who do not fit social norms.

Luke included the story of Jesus in the temple to point up his specialness and wisdom. This is how the child Jesus is shown on Eastern icons—a man in miniature, clad in royal robes, whose high-domed forehead represents infinite wisdom. In an age when we acknowledge that family life is far from easy, we identify with the fact that Jesus' parents were baffled and hurt by him.

I don't always understand Jesus either. I sympathize with Mary's reproaches and note that it's she, not Joseph, who reproves her gifted child. He had seemed lost and I often lose sight of him, too. However, Jesus was found safe within a place of prayer and this encourages me to keep on praying. Luke adds, 'His mother stored up all these things in her heart' (v. 51), giving us a character sketch of this woman in her home life in Nazareth.

Sunday reflection

Heavenly Father, whose blessed Son shared the life of an earthly home at Nazareth, make our homes places of love. Bless the education of our children and protect our families on our pilgrim way to your heavenly home.
Amen

JR

Tough love: letting go—and holding on

Then his brothers and his mother came, and standing outside they sent to him, calling him. And a multitude was sitting around him; and they said to him, 'Look, your mother and your brothers are outside seeking you.' But he... looked around in a circle at those who sat about him, and said, 'Here are my mother and my brothers! For whoever does the will of God is my brother and my sister and mother.'

Here's a tough passage! Mary is left outside with Jesus' brothers. Are these her birth sons? Christians are divided. Some point out that, in many societies, a first cousin counts as a brother. Others say that these are Joseph's sons, stepbrothers of Jesus, but whatever view we hold, Mary must learn that her eldest son has moved away from her. He is gathering a faith-family about him. One day he will draw her in, but in the meantime she must take second place.

Very often, love means letting go. That's tough, too. The sword of sorrow must have twisted in Mary's heart that day as his mother. She said 'yes' to the angel, she obeyed God and bore the promised child and now her son, whom some relatives have already tried to restrain, saying he's mad (v. 21), disowns her in front of the rag-tag crowd pressed about him.

Tough love means letting go. It also means hanging on. I think of a mother whose teenage son walked out and never returned.

His younger brother is in a locked hospital ward now, far from home. I think of a friend whose eldest child has a degenerating illness, whose middle child disappeared without trace and whose only grandchild has a rare, incurable disease. I think of parents shattered by marital breakdown while they struggle with an adult child's handicap. I watch Mary walk away from that house with sons (or stepsons) who don't believe in Jesus (John 7:5). Countless sermons are preached on doubting Thomas, Peter's faith and denial, but this passage is sometimes taken to show that Mary is no longer important in the story of faith. Not at all! I see mother Mary letting go, but holding on.

Prayer

Lord, let me hold on to you and please hold on to me and my loved ones, always. Amen

JR

Rejoice, ask, be filled!

I will greatly rejoice in the Lord... for he has clothed me with the garments of salvation... As a bridegroom decks himself with ornaments, and as a bride adorns herself with her jewels.

On the third day there was a wedding in Cana of Galilee, and the mother of Jesus was there... And when they ran out of wine, the mother of Jesus said to him, 'They have no wine.'

Mary's first appearance in John's Gospel is an incident charged with significance. It is 'the third day'—a symbol of the victory of the resurrection. The setting is a wedding, the symbol of God's union with his people, his salvation and generous forgiveness. Jesus refers to weddings or banquets at least six times in his parables.

Recently, a friend and her husband visiting Turkey were unexpectedly invited to a village wedding. Veiled women sat together. Musicians played. The foreign visitors were requested to dance. To make things worse, both were in shorts. The mindset of that wedding shows the protocol of the wedding at Cana—a protocol Mary was about to defy. Although she is mentioned before Jesus himself—evidence that John regards her position in the story as very significant—Mary would have been seated among the other women where she must have heard from the waiters' worried whispers that there was no wine left.

Anxious to save the situation, Mary leaves the women's side to speak to Jesus. As a guest, it was his job to do something. Bring your own bottle was the rule. Some commentators suggest that Jesus may have been too poor to have done the expected thing and bring supplies of wine. Whatever the reason, Mary states the problem and waits for Jesus to act.

We see in Mary the sensitivity to human need, the readiness to help and the willingness to break rules that characterized Jesus' ministry. We learn something about prayer and, since wine in scripture symbolizes the Holy Spirit, we see how we must ask God to keep filling us with power and love. The key is, as Mary knew, to rejoice in the Lord and trust his salvation.

Reflection

'They have no wine.' Ask God to uncork his best wine and pour it abundantly into your life today.

JR

Water of anxiety to wine of love

Jesus said to her, 'Woman, what does your concern have to do with me? My hour has not yet come.' His mother said to the servants, 'Whatever he says to you, do it.' Now there were set there six waterpots of stone... Jesus said to them, 'Fill the waterpots with water.' And they filled them up to the brim. And he said to them, 'Draw some out now, and take it to the master of the feast.'

Mary caused a stir when she went across to the men's side, but, in doing so, she made a public statement about her faith in her son's authority. Jesus' response seems cold—especially as his dealings with women are usually warm and compassionate. However, he only ever addresses two women by name—Martha (Luke 10:41) and Mary Magdalene (John 20:16). Also, this could have been a cultural thing. In parts of Asia and Africa, mothers are referred to—even by their husbands—as the mother of the eldest son. In Poland, even within the family, older people are addressed respectfully in the third person.

Even so, the Lord seems uncharacteristically grudging, but he explains by saying, 'My hour has not yet come.' The waterpots give us a clue, as seven is the number of perfection and, although they are filled to the brim, there are only six. Only when Jesus bows his head in death will all be complete. His mother will be there beside the cross, sharing in the loss and fulfilment of that 'hour'.

For now, however, Mary understands that, despite the domestic setting of a wedding, Jesus has moved beyond the demands of his human family. She has to let go of her claims as a mother on her son and follow him as her Lord. Her faith, humility and complete submission shine out as she tells the servants, 'Whatever he says to you, do it.' These are the words of life-changing faith. The result is the first recorded miracle in John's Gospel: Jesus changes water into wine and reveals his glory (John 2:1–11).

Mary shows us the secret of the power of prayer—naming the need and leaving the rest to God. It's very hard to do this, but I have noticed that people who pray this way possess peace.

Prayer

Lord, help me 'let go and let God'.
Change the water of my anxieties
into the wine of your abundant love.

JR

Disciples at the foot of the cross

Now there stood by the cross of Jesus his mother, and his mother's sister, Mary the wife of Clopas, and Mary Magdalene. When Jesus therefore saw his mother, and the disciple whom he loved standing by, he said to his mother, 'Woman, behold your son!' Then he said to the disciple, 'Behold your mother!' And from that hour that disciple took her to his own home.

The disciples had fled in terror when Jesus was arrested (Mark 14:50). However, the women stayed till the end, sharing his suffering and shame. Mary the disciple was with them. Mary the mother watched her son undergo a death so cruel that it was later banned as a form of execution. The sword Simeon prophesied has twisted in her heart many times already, but pierces it altogether now.

She is not alone, though. John, the disciple Jesus loved, is standing with the women beside the cross. With his dying breath, Jesus gives his mother into the care of his dear friend, although Mary has other close male relatives (Mark 3:31). Perhaps the brothers of Jesus were too poor to care for Mary the widow. Perhaps, quite simply they didn't believe in him (John 7:5). Whatever the reason, like the other male disciples, they are conspicuous by their absence at Calvary.

Broken-hearted, Mary and John will support each other. They both belong to the family of faith, the Church. What we make of this is a cause of division among Christians to this day. Many Reformed churches have tended to throw out the mother with the bathwater. I have come to realize that this has been a real spiritual impoverishment, although some forms of Catholicism seem to distort the faithful disciple whose pilgrim path we follow through the Gospels.

All Christians, however, see Mary at the foot of the cross as an affirmation for every suffering mother who grieves for her children's hurts. Mary's son can no longer reach out and touch her, but, for mother Mary, beloved John and, indeed, all of us who wait by the cross, he weaves the harsh threads of sorrow into a soft cloth of love and compassion.

Reflection

Sorrowing love turns the place of hurt into the place of repair.

JR

The saddest Sabbath

Joseph of Arimathea, a prominent council member, who was him-self waiting for the kingdom of God... went in to Pilate and asked for the body of Jesus... Then he bought fine linen, took him down... And he laid him in a tomb which had been hewn out of the rock, and rolled a stone against the door of the tomb. And Mary Magdalene and Mary the mother of Joses observed where he was laid.

Was 'our' Mary with the other grieving women who tucked oint-ments and wild herbs of Galilee into the folds of the shroud? Even if Mary is not the 'mother of Joses' (named in Mark 6:3 as one of the brothers of Jesus), it is hardly likely that she would have gone home with John, leaving the other women, close relatives and sisters in sorrow. I am sure she would have gone with them, a sad, bro-ken procession to watch the men lay the body of Jesus in the rock tomb and roll that heavy stone in front of the grave.

Christ who, as the Orthodox liturgy says, was clothed in light as with a garment (Psalm 104:2) is now wrapped in a shroud. There was no time to embalm the body as the sabbath was about to begin. As soon as it ended, the women would set to work all night on their last act of sorrowing love, preparing spices to bring to the grave at break of day. The Orthodox liturgy celebrates the Feast of the Myrrh-bearing women —these quiet, veiled figures who brave the darkness and the guards because they love Jesus and are the first witnesses to his resurrection.

Mary's story began among hid-den people and she is with them still. Joseph of Arimathea, rich and important as he was, is also one of God's humble people who hopes for the Kingdom to come. His hope and hers are fulfilled beyond all expectations, but first they had to endure the saddest sabbath of all. Life is asleep, says an Orthodox prayer; the one who holds creation in the palm of his hands lies hid-den in the darkness of a grave.

Prayer

Bury my failure and darkness within your grave, O Lord, so that with the faithful women I may welcome res-urrection light beyond all pain.
Amen

JR

The last milestone

He was seen by over 500 brethren at once… by James, then by all the apostles.

Then they returned to Jerusalem… And when they had entered, they went up into the upper room where they were staying… [The 11 disciples] all continued with one accord in prayer and supplication, with the women and Mary the mother of Jesus, and with his brothers.

Gradually the tremendous truth dawned as the risen Lord appeared to his disciples, family and kinsfolk. Brother James became a leader in the church in Jerusalem (Acts 12:17; Galatians 1:19), but no one could claim blood ties any more. There is a new family of faith and into it the Lord's brothers, believing at last, are drawn.

So we come to the upper room —probably the home of John Mark's mother (Acts 12:12). Former misunderstandings are forgotten as the fishermen and the women, the kinsfolk of Jesus and his friends pray together for the Holy Spirit, just as the Lord had told them. This is the last time Mary appears in the New Testament. Let's recall the landmarks on her pilgrimage. Mary belongs to the 'meek and humble people' of Israel. Her 'yes' changes the course of history. Then, Elizabeth, filled with the Holy Spirit, acknowledges Mary's as yet hidden pregnancy. In Mary's great song of praise, she hallows God's name—a life-changing prayer. Then, she bears the Son of God and receives the blessing of sorrow. She learns that tough love means letting go and holding on. Sensitive and ready to help, her trust in Jesus shows us the secret power of prayer and the Lord reveals his glory. Mary is faithful to the end and is drawn into the faith-family, the Church.

We, too, must say 'yes' to God, rejoice, hallow his name and bear Christ within us. We must hold on during dark times so that the place of hurt becomes the place of repair. We, too, belong to the faith-family, with blessings to sustain us on our pilgrim way.

Prayer

Lord, you chose a humble home and your blessed mother witnessed your passion and your resurrection glory. Together with her, we worship you, Mary's child, only Son of the Father, world without end. Amen

JR

Titles of a holy God

'What's in a name?' people ask, and Shakespeare claimed that 'a rose by any other name would smell as sweet'. He's probably right, but, nevertheless, names are important. Think of the effort put into choosing the name of a new baby. Names in that other sense of titles or nicknames can also tell us a lot about a person's attributes. Think of Ethelred the Unready, Richard the Lionheart or, more recently, Eddy the Eagle!

In the Bible, names are very important because, in Hebrew thought, a name represents your character. Many people were renamed after an important event in their lives—Abraham, Peter, Paul, to name but three. As we reflect on the names and titles of God in the Old Testament, we shall see that each of them tells us something about the complexity and depth of wisdom that mark our holy and eternal God.

In fact, God only has two 'names'—in the sense of 'official titles'—in Hebrew, *Elohim* (God), and *Yahweh* or 'Jehovah' (I am). One tells us who God is—I am, the eternal one. The other tells us his 'role', what he does—almighty God, creator and sustainer of the universe. As a Jewish comedian once put it rather neatly, 'Jehovah's his name, God's his occupation'!

The other names we shall be looking at are really nicknames, if that doesn't sound too irreverent. Some were coined by people after particular experiences that enabled them to discover more about God. Some came by a revelation in a vision or moment of insight. Some were attached to places where God had done a mighty deed. However they came about, they became part of the religious experience of the ancient people of God and they have often brought inspiration to more recent Christians, too.

Over the next few days, we shall be looking at some of those names. The ideas they convey are absolutely fundamental to our understanding of God as majestic, unchanging, the giver of good gifts and the protector of his people. All of this may help us to understand more fully why we value the name by which Christians most commonly know him—'Father'. There is also, of course, what Paul called 'the name above every name'—'Jesus', 'Saviour' (one of the Old Testament titles of God). At that name, we are told, 'every knee shall bow'.

David Winter

Almighty God

In the beginning when God created the heavens and the earth, the earth was a formless void and darkness covered the face of the deep, while a wind from God swept over the face of the waters. Then God said, 'Let there be light'; and there was light. And God saw that the light was good; and God separated the light from the darkness. God called the light Day, and the darkness he called Night. And there was evening and there was morning, the first day.

This beautiful piece of poetry, introducing the creation story, to all intents and purposes begins with God. It does not argue for his existence, but assumes that it is entirely self-evident: 'In the beginning, God...' The word used here for God is, in Hebrew, *Elohim* and it is one of the two divine names in scripture. The other, as we shall see tomorrow, is *Yahweh*, I am. It is the plural form of the common word for 'god' (as in, for instance, 'the gods of the heathen'), but using that multiplication, as it were, indicates that this is the God above all gods or, as we put it, simply 'almighty God'.

This passage emphasizes his most fundamental characteristic—he is the creator of the universe and, hence, all living things, including human beings. We are made in his image, not—as the Jews liked to point out—he in ours, as was the case for the gods of many of the pagan cultures around them. He is also the creator, rather than simply the maker. This distinction is quite important. A maker takes what already exists —wood, glue, nails—and fashions something from it—a chair, perhaps. A creator is more like a composer of music. Beethoven sat at a piano and the Seventh Symphony didn't exist in any form at all but from his own imagination and will it emerged—in a real sense, something from nothing, his own unique and original creation. It is in that sense that God is the Creator, bringing into existence from nothing all that is. What a thought!

Sunday reflection

'It is he that made us, and we are his; we are his people, and the sheep of his pasture' (Psalm 100:3).

DW

Yahweh, I am

But Moses said to God, 'If I come to the Israelites and say to them, "The God of your ancestors has sent me to you", and they ask me, "What is his name?" what shall I say to them?' God said to Moses, 'I am who I am.' He said further, 'Thus you shall say to the Israelites, "I am has sent me to you."' God also said to Moses, 'Thus you shall say to the Israelites, "The Lord, the God of your ancestors, the God of Abraham, the God of Isaac, and the God of Jacob, has sent me to you": This is my name forever, and this my title for all generations.'

Moses already knew the holy name—at any rate, Abraham his ancestor knew it and it had been used since as a title of God. What he didn't know was its meaning and it is this that is the great revelation of the burning bush story—the story of which this is a part. If Moses were to go to Egypt to rescue his people and say that 'the God of their fathers' had sent him, he didn't feel that it would be enough to recite the holy name as his authority. What God revealed to him was the profundity of that title. 'I am who I am' expands on the shorter title *Yahweh*, meaning simply 'I am'. In fact, it plays on various elements of the Hebrew verb 'to be', making the point that God is not this or that, but all that is. (The more familiar version of this name is 'Jehovah', which scholars now suggest was an inaccurate transliteration of the letters 'YHWH', used to conceal the divine name.) That was the nature of the God who sent Moses and would deliver them from slavery.

Human life is usually summed up in three tenses. We were born, at a point in time; we are alive, now; and at a later point in time we shall die. We experience past, present and future. The holy name, however, tells us that God is beyond time, without beginning or end, a permanent present tense: 'I am'. It is in this eternal God that we put our trust.

Reflection

Change and decay in all around I see; O Thou who changest not, abide with me.

H.F. Lyte (1793–1847)
DW

The Lord of hosts

But David said to the Philistine, 'You come to me with sword and spear and javelin; but I come to you in the name of the Lord of hosts, the God of the armies of Israel, whom you have defied. This very day the Lord will deliver you into my hand, and I will strike you down... so that all the earth may know that there is a God in Israel, and that all this assembly may know that the Lord does not save by sword and spear; for the battle is the Lord's and he will give you into our hand.'

The first of the divine titles we shall be looking at (as distinct from the two divine names) is 'Lord of hosts', which in Hebrew is *El Sabaoth*. It was a title much favoured in the history books of Israel, where God is seen as the captain of the armies of God's chosen people. However, as here, he is much more than that. After all, as David well knew, at that moment, the 'army of God's chosen people' was cowering at the spectacle of the Philistine giant waving his mighty spear. David was calling on the captain of a greater, and as yet invisible host, who would enable an apparently unarmed boy to defeat this blaspheming enemy.

We tend to praise David for his courage and dexterity with a sling, and that is fair enough. He was a brave young man. However, as he stood there before Goliath, it was not his skill or experience in killing wild beasts that mattered most. He knew precisely where help would come from—*El Sabaoth*, the 'Lord of hosts'. That unseen army of the skies would ensure that God's enemies were defeated.

It's a lesson we all need to take on board. There's a lovely story in the life of the prophet Elisha of a time when he comforts a young man who is fearful in the face of the enemy chariots with a sudden revelation of the presence of an angelic army on the hills around them. There are moments when we all need the reassurance that 'the Lord of hosts is with us, the God of Jacob is our refuge' (Psalm 46:7).

Reflection

'Do not be afraid, for there are more with us than there are with them'
(2 Kings 6:16).

DW

The Lord is there

He brought me, in visions of God, to the land of Israel, and set me down upon a very high mountain, on which was a structure like a city to the south. When he brought me there, a man was there, whose appearance shone like bronze, with a linen cord and a measuring reed in his hand; and he was standing in the gateway... The circumference of the city shall be 18,000 cubits. And the name of the city from that time on shall be, The Lord is There.

Our passage spans the beginning and end of the final vision of the very visionary book of Ezekiel. A man (or is he an angel?) shows the prophet the future for God's people, living in a land of peace and holiness, centred on the worship at the temple. However, it is the very last word that is the best. The heavenly city—and that is what it is, the 'new Jerusalem'—has a name and it is yet another name for God: The Lord is There, *Yahweh-Shammah*.

Christians may well compare this to the vision at the end of the New Testament, in the book of Revelation, where the heavenly city is described in similar terms, but now with the Lord God and the 'Lamb' (Jesus) at the heart of it. This is what makes heaven, heaven—the Lord is there. The God who accompanied the people of Israel through the wilderness, the God who is with his people as they walk through 'the valley of the shadow of death' (Psalm 23:4, NKJV) and the God who shared our humanity in his Son Jesus (John 1:14), will at the last be the centre of our lives for ever.

Yahweh-Shammah is the name that speaks of the God who is present and there is no greater source of comfort, as many of us could testify. God doesn't promise to take all the nasty bits out of our lives, but he does promise to be with us through everything. Nothing is more important than that. Whatever comes, whatever happens, the Lord is there!

Reflection

The name 'Emmanuel' means 'God is with us' (Matthew 1:23). Jesus promised his disciples that he would be with them 'always, to the end of the age' (Matthew 28:20). The Lord is there—Yahweh-Shammah!

DW

The Lord will provide

But the angel of the Lord called to him from heaven, and said, 'Abraham, Abraham!' And he said, 'Here I am.' He said, 'Do not lay your hand on the boy or do anything to him; for now I know that you fear God, since you have not withheld your son, your only son, from me.' And Abraham looked up and saw a ram, caught in a thicket by its horns. Abraham went and took the ram and offered it up as a burnt offering instead of his son. So Abraham called that place 'the Lord will provide'; as it is said to this day, 'On the mount of the Lord it shall be provided.'

In this rather strange story (to modern thinking, at least) one thing seems clear—God never intended harm to come to Isaac. His test of Abraham's faith involved the person dearest to him, but, at the crucial moment, another offering was provided in place of the boy. Full of joy at the discovery, Abraham gave the place a name, one that became another of those divine 'nicknames' to the people of Israel: *Yahweh-Jireh*, which means 'the Lord will provide'.

It has become a very precious title to succeeding generations of not only Jewish people, but also Christian believers. There are chapels in the Welsh hills dedicated to 'Jehovah Jireh', sometimes because in the days of revival the Lord did indeed 'provide' the funds from a poor congregation to build themselves a place of worship. Missionaries in moments of need, Christians wondering where the next meal would come from, lonely hearts crying out for companionship—all have found with joy that this ancient name still rings true. Also, he provided on Golgotha a sacrifice for our sins in the person of his only Son.

The Lord does provide—not everything we want, of course, but all that we truly need. Just as he provided for his people on that long journey across the wilderness—manna and quail to eat, sweet water to drink, protection from their enemies—so he provides for his people today.

Reflection

'How much more will your Father in heaven give good things to those who ask him!' (Matthew 7:11)

DW

God of might

How happy is the one whom God reproves; therefore do not despise the discipline of the Almighty. For he wounds, but he binds up; he strikes, but his hands heal. He will deliver you from six troubles; in seven no harm shall touch you. In famine he will redeem you from death, and in war from the power of the sword.

The title for God that we shall reflect on today is *El Shaddai*, 'the mighty one'. This is a particularly common name for God in the book of Job, which can be seen as an exercise in conveying both the discipline and mercy of the Lord. This title reminds us that nothing happens beyond the controlling power of God, whether it be sad or happy, beautiful or ugly, wounding or healing. That is not to say that God directly causes each detail of life—that would rob us of any freedom of will, one of his creation gifts to us—but he is at work in and through everything that happens. Paul caught it very precisely in Romans 8:28 (NIV): 'And we know that in all things God works for the good of those who love him…' (literally).

In this passage from Job, in which one of his 'comforters', Eliphaz the Temanite, is speaking, the man weighed down with grief and sorrow is reminded that even if this is to be seen in some way as a 'discipline', nevertheless the one who wounds will also 'bind up' and the hands that struck him down are also hands of healing. Job's comforters are not, as it happens, able to answer his deepest questions about God and suffering, but that doesn't mean that there isn't wisdom in what they say. It is always and everywhere true that 'the mighty one' knows our circumstances, personality, needs and weaknesses. He wounds and he binds up.

All of this is what the name *El Shaddai* meant to the people of the old covenant. This is the name that told them that God was in ultimate control, that the King of kings was on his throne!

Reflection

We do not live in a universe without government and we are at the mercy of neither fate nor human whim.

DW

The Lord is peace

Then Gideon perceived that it was the angel of the Lord; and Gideon said, 'Help me, Lord God! For I have seen the angel of the Lord face to face.' But the Lord said to him, 'Peace be to you; do not fear, you shall not die.' Then Gideon built an altar there to the Lord, and called it, The Lord is peace. To this day it still stands at Ophrah, which belongs to the Abiezrites.

Many translations of the Bible help the reader by indicating that the name *Yahweh* (Jehovah) is being used by printing 'the Lord' in capital letters. The other divine name, as we have seen, is *Elohim*, usually translated as 'God' or 'Almighty God' or 'the Lord' (without capitals). The 'extra' name we are considering today is a combination of *Yahweh* and *Shalom*—the Hebrew word for peace. When Gideon was terrified because he thought he had met the 'angel'—'presence'—of *Yahweh* face to face, the Lord reassured him with words of peace. This so impressed Gideon that he built an altar at the spot and called it 'The Lord is Peace'.

Down the centuries, that has been the constant experience of believers. Peace is not best bought either by compromise or conquest, but received as a gift. The Lord, who is peace, gives peace.

You may recall the words of peace that the risen Jesus spoke to the disciples (John 20:19 and 21), but also think of the peace that he brought to the terrified sailors in the storm on the lake (Mark 4:39) and to the restored demoniac (Mark 5:15). Think also of Paul who spoke of Jesus 'making peace through the blood of his cross' (Colossians 1:20) and of 'the God of peace' (Philippians 4:9), echoing this lovely title from Hebrew scriptures.

It is all too easy to think of God as referred to in the Old Testament as 'Lord of battles' and contrast him with the God of peace who is the Father of Jesus. However, this is a false distinction. *Yahweh-Shalom* offers no easy compromise, it is true, and no soft options, but the peace he offers is real and eternal.

Reflection

'The peace of God, which surpasses all understanding' is the gift; the 'God of peace' is the giver (Philippians 4:4–9).

DW

117

Easter: Mark's Gospel and Peter

Mark's Gospel is considered to be the earliest of the four Gospels in the New Testament. One of Mark's favourite words is 'immediately', which can be translated in a variety of ways, such as 'then', 'next' and so forth. In today's parlance, we might well describe this Gospel as 'in your face'—the narrative is fast-moving, there is less room for the teaching of Jesus and such teaching is often given as part of a conflict situation anyway. Another feature of Mark's Gospel is that Jesus' identity is enigmatic. While the demons might recognize that he is the Son of God, the religious leaders certainly don't and the disciples mainly miss the truth as well.

There is also the sense that we are glimpsing events via an eyewitness. For instance, from time to time we get details that are difficult to explain otherwise. This supports the view, which goes back to very early times, that Mark wrote down what he heard about Jesus from Peter. We shall use this insight for the post Easter readings, which will explore the impact of Christ's resurrection in 1 Peter chapters 1—3. It is worth noting, too, that Peter refers to Mark being with him (1 Peter 5:13).

However, before the resurrection there is the darkness of the crucifixion and Passion week, which precedes it. All the Gospels give a high percentage of their space to these events (after all, it was only one week out of possibly three years in the ministry of Jesus). In Mark, this is even more accentuated, surely indicating that the early Christians recognized that all the issues, human and divine, that were played out in the life of Jesus receive their clearest focus and resolution in these events.

As we read these chapters, we see a pattern of darkness and light (for darkness see Mark 14:1–2, 10–11, 17–21, 27–31; for light 14:3–9, 12–16, 22–26). It then becomes unrelieved darkness until after the death of Jesus on the cross. Then, slowly, first with Joseph of Arimathea, then with the devotion of the women who go to the tomb, the first glimmers of dawn return, culminating in the bright flash of the first resurrection news, which leaves the women 'awestruck'.

We, however, will focus on characters who, by virtue of their interaction with Jesus, illuminate his significance for the world.

David Spriggs

Jesus and the woman—an open heart

Jesus was eating in Bethany at the home of Simon, who once had leprosy, when a woman came in with a very expensive bottle of sweet-smelling perfume. After breaking it open, she poured the perfume on Jesus' head. This made some of the guests angry, and they complained, 'Why such a waste?' ... But Jesus said: 'Leave her alone! Why are you bothering her? She has done a beautiful thing for me... She has done all she could by pouring perfume on my body to prepare it for burial. You may be sure that wherever the good news is told all over the world, people will remember what she has done. And they will tell others.'

Why spend large amounts of money on cosmetics and perfumes? The answer of one company is, 'Because you're worth it'. Why did this nameless woman pour profligate amounts of perfumed oil over Jesus? Not because she felt she was worth it, but because she was sure Jesus was.

It is intriguing to speculate what prompted her to carry out this audacious and apparently superfluous act. The similar story in Luke (7:36–50) suggests that it was overflowing love, prompted by a deep and transforming experience of forgiveness that Jesus brought her. The account in John (12:1–8) implies that it was out of Mary's deep gratitude for all that Jesus had done for her brother and the household. However, in Mark's account there is no emotion and no explanation—from the woman's side!

Mark focuses on the meaning this act has for Jesus. He sees in her total generosity that she is doing a 'beautiful thing for me' (v. 6). He sees her action as an embalming—'pouring perfume on my body to prepare it for burial'. She is anointing the Messiah (note the perfume is poured on Jesus' head, not his feet (v. 3). Like the entry into Jerusalem, this woman is announcing to the world who Jesus is and what will happen to him. Not only her generosity, but her public declaration, did indeed ensure that her story is still told and will be told always.

For further reading, see Mark 14:3–9.

Sunday reflection

Lord Jesus, give to us the open heart of generous love that demonstrates to all the meaning of your cross.

DS

Jesus and the man—an open home

It was the first day of the Festival of Thin Bread, and the Passover lambs were being killed. Jesus' disciples asked him, 'Where do you want us to prepare the Passover meal?' Jesus said to two of the disciples, 'Go into the city, where you will meet a man carrying a jar of water. Follow him, and when he goes into a house, say to the owner, "Our teacher wants to know if you have a room where he can eat the Passover meal with his disciples."' ... The two disciples went into the city and found everything just as Jesus had told them. So they prepared the Passover meal.

The woman of yesterday's passage may have acted spontaneously or been planning her act of love for weeks, we do not know. We can be sure, however, that the man who owned the home where Jesus would celebrate his last Passover had been thinking things through carefully. Whether Jesus approached him or the man perceived that Jesus would have such requirements and offered, again, we don't know. What we do know is that he was willing to provide an open home for Jesus, and such an invitation was becoming a courageous and costly thing to do. Thus, a degree of secrecy was required, hence the special arrangements of the man carrying the water pot whom the disciples were to follow to their secret location. The courage and the cost were increased because clearly the man was wealthy —it was a large room (v. 15).

The woman in our reading yesterday was preparing Jesus and all who could see for the Passion, his suffering. The man we meet today was enabling Jesus to prepare his disciples for the Passion. Each, in very different ways, showed commitment that meant taking a risk.

The woman's gift could only be given once; the man could use his room again. Sometimes our devotion to Christ means we give something up for ever, sometimes we can go on using it for ourselves. Both kinds of giving can be used by Jesus to share the significance of the Passion with others.

For further reading, see Mark 14:12–16.

Reflection

When have I given like the woman—superfluously and unrepeatably? Or like the man—practically and temporarily? How can my giving this week proclaim the meaning of Jesus and his death to others?

DS

Jesus and Judas

It was now two days before Passover and the Festival of Thin Bread. The chief priests and the teachers of the Law of Moses were secretly planning to have Jesus arrested and put to death. They were saying, 'We must not do it during the festival, because the people will riot.' ... Judas Iscariot was one of the twelve disciples. He went to the chief priests and offered to help them arrest Jesus. They were glad to hear this, and they promised to pay him. So Judas started looking for a good chance to betray Jesus.

So far, we have met an unnamed woman and an unnamed man, but this disciple's name has gone down in history and is synonymous with betrayal and intrigue—Judas Iscariot. As Jesus said 'That man would be better off if he had never been born' (v. 21).

Why did he do it? Jealousy, ambition and a desire to force Jesus to stir up revolt against the Romans have been suggested, but his motive remains speculative. Perhaps avarice played a part, as Matthew 26:15 suggests, but Mark gives us no clue here. In the end, there is neither explanation nor justification on the human level of motivation. The point is, it happened and it happened to Jesus.

So, when we learn of unbelievable cruelty or experience dreadful betrayals, we need to place them alongside this story from the Passion. This is not to diminish our pain or the gruesome consequences. Indeed, it is this very story that reveals the abysmal depths to which human nature can sink. To bring our torments here is important, for we discover in the presence of Jesus that we do not need to despair, either of other people or final outcomes because even this darkest of dark acts did not thwart the loving purposes of God.

There is one more thing this story challenges us to do—search our hearts and ensure that our discipleship and devotion do not turn to twisted betrayal.

For further reading, see Mark 14:43–49.

Prayer

Lord Jesus, thank you that even though you knew that Judas would betray you, you still treated him with courtesy and love. Help us to walk this way with you, especially when we feel betrayed—by parents, children, partner, employer or friend. Amen

DS

Jesus and Peter

Jesus went with his disciples to a place called Gethsemane, and he told them, 'Sit here while I pray.' Jesus took along Peter, James, and John. He was sad and troubled and told them, 'I am so sad that I feel as if I am dying. Stay here and keep awake with me.' Jesus walked on a little way. Then he knelt down on the ground and prayed, 'Father, if it is possible, don't let this happen to me! Father, you can do anything. Don't make me suffer by making me drink from this cup. But do what you want, and not what I want.' When Jesus came back and found the disciples sleeping, he said to Simon Peter, 'Are you asleep? Can't you stay awake for just one hour? Stay awake and pray that you won't be tested. You want to do what is right, but you are weak.' Jesus went back and prayed the same prayer.

Jesus was no stoic! Not for him the stiff upper lip that seeks to hide the stress and pain from others, nor the self-imposed exile to deal with grief alone. Jesus was fully human and so experienced deep anxiety as he imagined the horrors of the coming mock trials and gruesome death becoming reality. 'I am so sad that I feel as if I am dying', he said to Peter, James and John (v. 33). He was fully human in wanting his closest friends as near as possible as he attempted to deal with his profound fears— 'Stay here and keep awake with me' (v. 34).

Being fully human means we need to wrestle with God as well as with our fears. This, too, Mark shows us clearly. Such resolution of our anxieties is not arrived at without cost and perseverance, for Jesus has to repeat the process, nor is it arrived at without God.

In the garden, in the darkness of a Passover night, Jesus prepared himself as far as he could for the ordeal of the Passion. Even the desertion by his friends, especially Peter (see v. 37), was part of this process.

Eventually, all that preparation could do was accomplished and the time to live the death itself arrived—'The time has come' (v. 41).

Prayer

Help us, Lord Jesus, to watch with you. Amen

DS

Jesus and the high priest

Jesus was led off to the high priest. Then the chief priests, the nation's leaders, and the teachers of the Law of Moses all met together... The chief priests and the whole council tried to find someone to accuse Jesus of a crime, so they could put him to death. But they could not find anyone to accuse him. Many people did tell lies against Jesus, but they did not agree on what they said... The high priest stood up in the council... But Jesus... did not say a word. The high priest asked him... 'Are you the Messiah, the Son of the glorious God?' 'Yes, I am!' Jesus answered. 'Soon you will see the Son of Man sitting at the right side of God all-powerful, and coming with the clouds of heaven.'

The high priest, as befits such a person, bided his time. The leading priests and members of the Jewish council, the Sanhedrin, were desperate to establish the guilt of Jesus for a capital offence. They scurried about in the early hours to produce witnesses. People were willing to say almost anything to oblige (whether out of fear or hope of financial gain is not stated), but their attempts failed miserably.

The whole council was getting desperate and we sense mounting panic in Mark's narrative until 'The high priest stood up'. Like the lion who senses that the prey is wearied by the relentless chase, so the high priest saw his chance. He probed, seeking to provoke Jesus to speak in his own defence, but Jesus remained silent, thus refusing to acknowledge the legitimacy of this improperly convened court. Then came the stroke of genius. 'Are you the Messiah, the son of the glorious God?'

The council would have used silence as a denial by Jesus of his Messiahship, so Jesus had to acknowledge the truth of the high priest's words. The lion pounced. He tore his robes—an indication of blasphemy—and all agreed that Jesus must die (vv. 63–64).

For further reading, see 14:53–64.

Prayer

Lord Jesus, thank you that you were willing to endure such mockery and injustice. Please help us to see where hypocrisy and self-interest blind us and all who are in the Church to prejudice and injustice. Save us from using our abilities to distort the truth and oppress the weak. Amen

DS

Jesus and Pilate

The chief priests brought many charges against Jesus. Then Pilate questioned him again, 'Don't you have anything to say? Don't you hear what crimes they say you have done?' But Jesus did not answer, and Pilate was amazed. During Passover, Pilate always freed one prisoner chosen by the people. And at that time there was a prisoner named Barabbas. He and some others had been arrested for murder during a riot.

Having so cleverly accused Jesus of being the Messiah, the Sanhedrin had one small problem left. They could not carry out the death sentence and Pilate was not going to regard a religious claim of blasphemy as of any interest to Rome.

However, while Jesus' claim to be the Messiah and Son of God was enough for the Jews, the claim to be the Messiah and therefore a king should be enough for Pilate. Here was the real genius of the high priest's lunge. Pilate, though, seemed unconvinced.

Pilate could not lure Jesus into personally confessing that he was the Jewish king, nor could Pilate persuade him to answer the myriad accusations that were being thrown at him by the priests. Something about Jesus clearly impressed itself on Pilate, though, who 'was amazed'. He was also trapped between the pressure of the priests (a powerful force in Jerusalem and, through their networks, across much of the Roman Empire) and the pressure of the truth.

So, Pilate sought to escape from his dilemma by affirming a Jewish custom of releasing a prisoner at Passover. It was a neat ploy as, implicitly, to release Jesus in this way would affirm his guilt but also affirm the justice of Rome. Unfortunately, Pilate was caught in his own trap by the cry of the crowd—'Nail him to a cross!' (v. 13). The result? Barabbas, a real threat to Roman stability, would be loosed and an innocent man would be put to death.

For further reading, see Mark 15:1–21.

Prayer

Lord Jesus, thank you that you show us the integrity of innocence and the strength of weakness even within a corrupt and corrupting power system. Help us, when we are faced with such complex systems at work, in commerce or politics to know how to live like you. Amen

DS

Jesus and Joseph of Arimathea

A man named Joseph from Arimathea was brave enough to ask Pilate for the body of Jesus. Joseph was a highly respected member of the Jewish council, and he was also waiting for God's kingdom to come. Pilate was surprised to hear that Jesus was already dead, and he called in the army officer to find out if Jesus had been dead very long. After the officer told him, Pilate let Joseph have Jesus' body.

The long day was over. For the priests with their scheming, Pilate with his tormenting dilemmas, the soldiers who supervised the prisoners from jail to crucifixion, the disciples in their paralysis of helplessness and Jesus, who had gone from the dark of the garden, through the dark of desertion to the darkness of death.

For Pilate, that death had come unexpectedly quickly. So quickly, that when a distinguished-looking Jew named Joseph, who came from Arimathea, asked for permission to bury the body before the sabbath began, Pilate summoned the centurion in charge of the crucifixion to make sure Jesus really was dead. He didn't want to leave anything to chance or rumour—there had been enough trouble with talk about John the Baptist reappearing. However, Jesus was dead, so Joseph received the permission he required.

Strange, isn't it? Among the disciples there was a Judas and within the very council that perverted justice to do away with Jesus there was a Joseph. He was 'waiting for God's kingdom to come' and, apparently, a secret disciple (John 19:38). He could not save Jesus from crucifixion, but he could honour him in his death. It must have taken a great deal of courage for Joseph to go to Pilate and even more to challenge the high priest and the whole council.

Already the cross is doing its work. A centurion sees who Jesus really is (15:39) and a secret believer comes out. Who knows where it will end.

For further reading, see Mark 15:22–27.

Prayer

Lord Jesus, thank you that you have endured the long dark day of dying. Thank you that you know its intense loneliness as well as its pain. Thank you that you have experienced its vulnerability as well as its mystery. Help us, like Joseph, to gain courage from your final journey. Amen

DS

MARK 16:1–4 (CEV)

Jesus and the women

After the sabbath, Mary Magdalene, Salome, and Mary the mother of James bought some spices to put on Jesus' body. Very early on Sunday morning, just as the sun was coming up, they went to the tomb. On their way, they were asking one another, 'Who will roll the stone away from the entrance for us?' But when they looked, they saw that the stone had already been rolled away. And it was a huge stone!

Mark's Easter story is a story of three women—'Mary Magdalene, Salome, and Mary the mother of James'. It is also the story of three puzzles.

Puzzle one—who will roll the stone away? This question perplexed the three brave and devoted women who made their way out of the city at first light to revisit the tomb, the burial place of Jesus. They had no doubt they could find the tomb as two of them had seen Joseph of Arimathea carry out the funeral rituals—apart from anointing the body with spices, which is what the women now came to do.

Puzzle two—who had rolled away the stone? Arriving at the burial cave, they immediately noticed that the stone was no longer in place. So puzzle one disappeared. When they looked in the cave, they saw a young man, described as an angel. He explained that God had raised Jesus to life and, hence, his body had gone. Then he commanded them to convey this message to the disciples.

Puzzle three—what happened next? We are told of the hasty departure and panic of the three women, but also that they 'were too afraid to tell anyone'. So how did the message of the resurrection get out and, more to the point, why did Mark finish his Gospel at this apparently 'dead end'?

There is no clear solution. We can speculate, we can even write up alternative endings, as the several variants show, but puzzles remain. Fortunately, three things are clear. First, it's true—Jesus is alive. Second, obviously the message did get out. Third, these two facts changed the disciples and the world. We are witnesses to that.

For further reading, see Mark 16:5–8 (and 9–16).

Sunday reflection

Thanks be to God who gives us victory through our Lord, Jesus Christ. Amen

DS

MARK 14:27–31 (CEV, ABRIDGED)

Jesus and Peter—you have been warned

Jesus said to his disciples, 'All of you will reject me...' Peter spoke up, 'Even if all the others reject you, I never will!' Jesus replied, 'This very night before a cock crows twice, you will say three times that you don't know me.' But Peter was so sure of himself that he said, 'Even if I have to die with you, I will never say that I don't know you!'

Peter was totally discredited. Jesus warned him that he would disown him three times on the night of his arrest, but—and here's a very telling thing—'Peter was so sure of himself' that he affirmed his willingness to die rather than deny Jesus. Then Jesus tried to prepare him for the coming turmoil in prayer (14:38), for he recognized that the inclination of Peter's heart was right as well as the weakness of his resolve. Peter, however, failed and failed and failed again.

Of course, in one sense, so did all the disciples, but they weren't the leader and they didn't fail so openly and so consistently. It should have been the end for Peter. How come it wasn't?

Jesus had known it would happen and still spoke positively of the future (14:28). Now the new future had arrived and with it a new future for Peter. So, the young man said to the three women, 'Now go and tell his disciples, and especially Peter, that he will go ahead of you to Galilee. You will see him there, just as he told you' (16:7).

There are two things to note for each of us. First, however badly we may mess things up, it does not need to be the end. Because of the resurrection, there is always the possibility of a new future for those who fall. Second, this process of restitution is not a reluctant one on God's part. Rather, like the father of the prodigal son, God in Christ comes running out to meet us. Like the shepherd, he comes to seek and save the lost.

For further reading, see Mark 14:53–72.

Prayer

Lord Jesus Christ, help us to experience the release of knowing that, because of the resurrection, defeat never needs to be the last word. Amen

DS

Peter and Jesus

The next morning the leaders, the elders, and the teachers of the Law of Moses met in Jerusalem… They brought in Peter and John and made them stand in the middle while they questioned them. They asked, 'By what power and in whose name have you done this?' Peter was filled with the Holy Spirit and told the nation's leaders and the elders: '… This man is standing here completely well because of the power of Jesus Christ from Nazareth. You put Jesus to death on a cross, but God raised him to life.' … The officials were amazed to see how brave Peter and John were, and they knew that these two apostles were only ordinary men… [who] had been with Jesus.

What a difference a few weeks can make. We might say this about the rapid development of a new baby or, even more likely, after someone has been very ill and required major surgery or of someone who had been unemployed for several months starting a job—their despair and lack of self-worth melting away. However, never have these words been more appropriate than when used to describe Peter.

A few weeks earlier, a servant girl (whose significance counted for very little in her world) had completely cowed Peter into rejecting any suggestion that he was associated with Jesus. Now, knowing full well that the Jewish leaders can be barbarically cruel, he is not only willing to be totally identified with Jesus, but also to confront those very leaders with their own crime.

Such amazing boldness (a word that is a mixture of clarity, conviction and courage) allows for only one explanation in the opinion of the council. Peter and his assistant John have been companions of Jesus. Somehow, as a result of the resurrection, Peter had been significantly changed. Yes, he would get things wrong again, but no, he would never disown Jesus.

For further reading, see Acts 4:1–31.

Prayer

Lord Jesus Christ, take our sins and forgive us, take our weaknesses and turn them into your strength, take our arrogance and turn it into divine boldness, for the glory of your name. Amen

DS

A living hope

Praise God, the Father of our Lord Jesus Christ. God is so good, and by raising Jesus from death, he has given us new life and a hope that lives on. God has something stored up for you in heaven, where it will never decay or be ruined or disappear. You have faith in God, whose power will protect you until the last day. Then he will save you, just as he has always planned to do. On that day you will be glad, even if you have to go through many hard trials for a while... You will be given praise and honour and glory when Jesus Christ returns.

The battle was over and a great victory had been won, but, for the Roman soldier, the return journey could be long, arduous, dangerous and demoralizing. What would keep the soldiers on track through the long journey home would be the knowledge that the emperor would welcome them with a triumphal entry into Rome. The thought of that homecoming would help to maintain discipline and morale.

For Peter, writing to Christians in Rome, the great victory of the resurrection shaped Christian living in a similar way. Life could be extremely tough, particularly if you were a slave or from the lower class, for oppression from your master or persecution from people disturbed by your moral stance were probable and hope of justice was scant. However, Christians had a new life—fresh with hope, brightened with joy, refreshed with love, whatever the outward circumstances. Even more than this, however, they were guaranteed a hero's welcome when they arrived home in heaven: God 'has given us new life and a hope that lives on' (v. 3).

We, too, need to focus on the 'praise and honour and glory' (v. 7) that are our promised reward. Some of us, because the going is tough, perhaps live with physical or emotional pain. To do so courageously and courteously requires constant diligence as well as the Holy Spirit's grace. Some of us need to keep our focus on the joy and glory of heaven, not so much because of the problems, but because of the perceived attractions around us—more of that tomorrow!

Prayer

Thanks be to God, who gives us this victory! Amen

DS

Living the new life

Be alert and think straight. Put all your hope in how kind God will be to you when Jesus Christ appears. Behave like obedient children. Don't let your lives be controlled by your desires, as they used to be. Always live as God's holy people should, because God is the one who chose you, and he is holy... So you must honour God while you live as strangers here on earth.

After a great victory in a distant part of the Roman Empire, the soldier on his journey home might discover a pleasant village and an attractive girl to settle down with. Equally, for us, as we travel towards our welcome in heaven, there are so many ways in which we can be pulled off track—pressures at work, living in an instant satisfaction culture, alternative moral behaviour, to name only three.

Hence, Peter tells his friends to live as 'strangers here on earth'. As Christians, our attitudes and behaviour need to be different, both in relation to the way we lived before we became Christians and the lifestyles of our neighbours and colleagues. Living as strangers is very hard when we live in a society where peer pressure is so strong. If we are young, we must drink Coca-Cola or wear Nike or their brand equivalents—it has to be 'the real thing'. If we are older, we must aspire to the top job and all the perks that go with it, whatever the personal and social disadvantages that may be hidden in that package.

There are three reasons Peter goes on to give for living as strangers. First, because we are to be like God, holy. Second, because of the high price paid for our freedom—namely, the sacrificial death of Christ. Third, because, as a result of the resurrection, we have been given new birth.

For further reading, see 1 Peter 1:18–25.

Reflection

Look carefully at your way of living, working, spending, use of leisure, the TV programmes you watch and so on to ensure that it truly honours God. Maybe, even more importantly, you could check out whether or not you are free to be different to those around you and ask God's help to live as one of his 'strangers' here.

DS

Rejects or specially chosen?

And now you are living stones that are being used to build a spiritual house. You are also a group of holy priests, and with the help of Jesus Christ you will offer sacrifices that please God. It is just as God says in the scriptures, 'Look! I am placing in Zion a choice and precious cornerstone. No one who has faith in that one will be disappointed.' You are followers of the Lord, and that stone is precious to you. But it isn't precious to those who refuse to follow him. They are the builders who tossed aside the stone that turned out to be the most important one of all.

Life could deal many blows to make people feel useless, undervalued or rejected. Slaves could be beaten or made to do the foulest of jobs for no reward. Women could be abused or ignored while their husbands went off to find their pleasures elsewhere. Men might be sent to fight with the legions, knowing their chances of returning were not great. Fear and powerlessness could dissolve self-worth. They still do and it is easy enough to think of similar situations in our world that can rob us of any sense of worth.

Peter reminds his friends that Jesus has been treated in these kinds of ways. He was the rejected one par excellence. However, the resurrection completely reversed human verdicts, with the glorious declaration of God that he has 'chosen and highly honoured' him (v. 4). He has been selected to be used not only to construct God's new temple, but also he is the precious cornerstone, the centre of the design and functionally the block that holds everything together.

In the same way, Peter encourages Christians to gain their own self-perspective from God—'you are living stones that are being used to build a spiritual house' (v. 5). Abused, misused, overlooked, overworked, taken for granted, taken for a ride, labelled as a failure, labelled as a freak—these are hard experiences to endure and rot our confidence, particularly if we live with them for months or years. However, we can rest assured that they are not God's verdict on us.

For further reading, see 1 Peter 2: 1–17.

Reflection

Consider the implications of Peter's challenge to see life from the perspective of Easter day for your own way of living—'Come to Jesus Christ'.

DS

The details—resurrection and work

Servants, you must obey your masters and always show respect to them. Do this, not only to those who are kind and thoughtful, but also to those who are cruel. God will bless you, even if others treat you unfairly for being loyal to him. You don't gain anything by being punished for some wrong you have done. But God will bless you, if you have to suffer for doing something good. After all, God chose you to suffer as you follow in the footsteps of Christ, who set an example by suffering for you.

Where and when did the view arise that the Christian faith was about Sunday observance or was somehow an easy option? Peter makes it unmistakably clear that being a Christian is the tough option for life in the workplace.

For many of his readers, the workplace was the household where they were slaves. As slaves, they could be beaten, sexually abused or exploited by their masters. For some slaves, there would be no respite from such treatment. Yet, these are the people who have been given a new life in the resurrection. It means that they are loved, they are valuable, they are to be holy, they do matter to God.

Equally, their attitudes to others, including their masters, matter to God. They are to be respectful, even if they are unfairly treated, because they are to imitate Christ in his sufferings. This is the ultimate motive for them and a powerful challenge to us, wherever we are in a relationship of service.

What can this mean? Teachers must show respect for even their most difficult pupils. Workers in a factory must be positive about, as well as towards, the managers, even if they are treated badly. Telesales operators need to remember that the abusive customer is a person with needs: they are called by God to honour even that customer in their hearts, and not only by using the standard patter. In the home, the challenge for us may well come in the shape of a disrespectful teenager. The promise for us all is 'God will bless you' and the reason Peter can be so sure is that God blessed Jesus by raising him from the dead.

For further reading, see 1 Peter 2:22–25.

Prayer
Lord, help me to live your way.
Amen

DS

Resurrection and marriage

If you are a wife, you must put your husband first. Even if he opposes our message, you will win him over by what you do. No one else will have to say anything to him, because he will see how you honour God and live a pure life. Don't depend on things like fancy hairstyles or gold jewellery or expensive clothes to make you look beautiful. Be beautiful in your heart by being gentle and quiet. This kind of beauty will last, and God considers it very special. If you are a husband, you should be thoughtful of your wife... Then nothing will stand in the way of your prayers.

Slavery was hard, but marriage could be also, particularly for the woman. Often the wife would have had no say in whom she married and had little protection once she was married. If she became a Christian, her situation could become more vulnerable still.

These verses challenge wives to put their husbands first, even if (perhaps especially if) they are not believers, and seek to win their approval by their dedication and purity. A beautiful character, rather than superficial beauty or fashion aids, are the key both to the heart of God and their husbands. For us, in days of gender equality, this challenge must surely apply to the husbands as much as the wives! Reliability, attentiveness, affirmation and understanding, not only the smart car or latest gadget, could well be the kind of thing Peter would ask of husbands now.

Perhaps more significant than the behaviour are the reasons we are to live differently. Our lifestyle and attitudes of heart in this most intimate and demanding of relationships will speak volumes to our partners (or close friends) about the reality (or otherwise) of our Christian faith. So, what are we saying? What we aspire to as the source of our attractiveness and value shows where our heart really is—so where is it?

Sundy reflection

Lord Jesus Christ, help me to show the awesome beauty of your resurrection in all my relationships, but especially my most intimate ones. Help me to do this, even when the relationship feels unrewarding and I am taken for granted. Amen

DS

Resurrection and everyday living

Don't be hateful and insult people just because they are hateful and insult you. Instead, treat everyone with kindness. You are God's chosen ones, and he will bless you. The scriptures say, 'Do you really love life? Do you want to be happy? Then stop saying cruel things and stop telling lies. Give up your evil ways and do right, as you find and follow the road that leads to peace...' Even if you have to suffer for doing good things, God will bless you. So stop being afraid and don't worry about what people might do.

Life can be tough. It just isn't true that 'words can never harm us'. People can say distressing things about us that can alienate us from our neighbours and make us intensely lonely. Equally, people can do dreadful things that can cause real damage to our property or even to us in body or mind. In one sense, we cannot guarantee that such harsh things will not happen (the crucifixion of Jesus should save us from any false security here). However, the greatest negative consequence of such treatment is within our control.

More serious than any pain or damage we might suffer is the danger that we might retaliate in kind and not with kindness (v. 9). More destructive than the experience itself is the possibility that we might be trapped in the fear that it might happen again (v. 14).

So, when a motorist cuts us up or our neighbour won't sort out their *Leylandii* or the mothers on the school run are spreading malicious rumours, we need to be careful to respond like Jesus. When we are overlooked or falsely accused at work, we need to handle it the Jesus way. Jesus did not waste unnecessary effort defending himself, nor did he utilize the energy he felt as anger with which to retaliate. Instead, he healed the ear of the man who came to arrest him and prayed for forgiveness on behalf of those who crucified him.

If we persist in doing good, then no one can stop God from blessing us.

Prayer

Lord Jesus Christ, as I reflect on your resurrection, help me believe in the reality of your blessing and live life accordingly. Amen

DS

Resurrection and ourselves

Honour Christ and let him be the lord of your life. Always be ready to give an answer when someone asks you about your hope. Give a kind and respectful answer and keep your conscience clear. This way you will make people ashamed for saying bad things about your good conduct as a follower of Christ. You are better off to obey God and suffer for doing right than to suffer for doing wrong.

'Honour Christ and let him be the lord of your life'—what a tremendous and stirring challenge for a new morning! How shall we do this? Much of the letter so far has been about our silent witness. Like Christ, we are to suffer without bitter retaliatory complaints, even when the suffering is, in fact, unjustified punishment imposed on us out of anger or jealousy. Wives are to win their husbands by the beauty of their lives, then words will be unnecessary, but this is not the whole Christian story.

There came a time in the trial when Jesus spoke out (Mark 14:62) and there will be a time for us, too. The cue is when people ask us about the hope that is in us. This hope is, of course, the hope born as a result of the resurrection (1 Peter 1:3). Normally, people will not phrase their questions as directly as 'Why are you so hopeful?' or even 'So what difference does Easter make?' They might say, however, 'Why do you put up with him/her?', 'Why do you not grumble like the rest of us?', 'Why don't you swear?' or 'Why are you so sympathetic/supportive?' Such questions are our opportunity to reveal that the risen Jesus is Lord of our lives and that his life, love, death and resurrection give us a different perspective on life, purpose in life and power for life.

For further reading, see 1 Peter 3:18–22.

Prayer

Lord Jesus Christ, help me to see the opportunities to share with others the secret that is within me. Thank you that, through your death and resurrection, you have given me a hope that lives on. Help me to be more aware of that hope making a difference in my life and so enjoy your companionship more myself.
Amen

DS

Resurrection and our gifts

Most important of all, you must sincerely love each other, because love wipes away many sins. Welcome people into your home and don't grumble about it. Each of you has been blessed with one of God's many wonderful gifts to be used in the service of others. So use your gift well. If you have the gift of speaking, preach God's message. If you have the gift of helping others, do it with the strength that God supplies. Everything should be done in a way that will bring honour to God because of Jesus Christ, who is glorious and powerful for ever. Amen

'Everything should be done in a way that will bring honour to God…' (v. 11). This passage gives us four key areas in which to apply its teaching: prayer, sincere love for other Christians, providing welcoming hospitality in our homes and using our spiritual gifts to serve others. In my experience, most Christians are good at one of these and struggle with the others.

For instance, perhaps you find prayer fairly easy. Praying alone, your enjoyment of God's presence and reality is increased and so your faith is rekindled. As you pray for other people, you sense that you have been involved in transforming the world. Perhaps you love to spend time praying with others, maybe in a small group or even through half a night in prayer with many hundreds.

Maybe you struggle with prayer, but providing lunches for students or helping to care for people at the night shelter that the churches have set up is just right for you. Seeing other people relaxed and restored may give you much satisfaction.

So, there are two challenges that this passage brings to us. First, we are challenged to affirm people who are different to ourselves in the way they most easily express their commitment to Christ—this is one element in sincerely loving them! Second, it challenges and encourages us to move beyond our comfort zones to explore another dimension of Christian living. After all, the resurrection blows away the boundaries of possibility and entices us into new ways of being.

For further reading, see 1 Peter 3:18–22.

Prayer

Lord Jesus Christ, help me to venture with you into new experiences of service. Keep my motives pure. Amen

DS

New Daylight

Magazine

wycliffe

'Jesus ordered his teachers to plant milk'

Peter Brassington

We can read the Bible every day and have a wide range of notes and resources to help us. Meanwhile, thousands of people groups are without a single verse of scripture in their language. One language that people thought couldn't be written is now in print, thanks to co-operation between several organizations, including Wycliffe Bible Translators. Now God's word, in the language of the Sabaot people, can be written on their hearts. Previously they did have access to a Bible in another language, but that doesn't always convey the message so clearly, as the heading above shows.

OK, so what that verse actually said was, 'Jesus ordered his disciples to enter the boat', but on Mount Elgon there are no boats. There's not much use for words like sea, lake, boat, fish, fisherman, or fishing nets. And because of this (and other linguistic difficulties) most Sabaot people understood the verse to say, 'Jesus ordered his teachers to plant milk.' That didn't make a whole lot of sense, and probably didn't encourage them to read the rest of the story.

This was one of the discoveries made twenty years ago in a survey to find out how well the Sabaot people of northern Kenya under-

> *And we thought that our people knew Swahili well!*

stood the Swahili 'Good News' New Testament. 'And we thought that our people knew Swahili well!' commented a local headmaster who was involved in carrying out the survey.

Testing a second passage, the survey team realized that the people had no understanding at all of the Swahili words for biblical concepts such as mercy or grace. They did know market Swahili quite well, but just because you know how to trade using another language, it doesn't mean you know the kinds of words used in the Bible. Today the Sabaot people read these passages in their own language!

Until there was a written form of Sabaot, God only ever spoke through the Bible in someone else's language. This made the meaning hard to understand and also raised uncomfortable questions for the Sabaots. Was theirs an important language? It was a language neither of education nor of the church. Were they an important people? Could God understand them when they prayed in Sabaot? Did he listen?

While others worried, Sammy Ndiwa and a small group of Sabaot elders decided to walk fifty miles to Nairobi to ask the Bible Society for help. A few weeks later, they were invited to attend a meeting with representatives from related language groups about 100 miles from where they lived.

Once he'd walked the fifty miles back to his home on Mount Elgon, Sammy asked the chief for a small amount of money to pay for his travel to the meeting. Sammy had almost no education and the chief didn't feel he could handle the meeting. He offered Sammy a compromise: 'I'll lend you some cows so you can plough your fields and plant maize.'

With more determination than confidence, Sammy decided to walk the 100 miles to the meeting. He was afraid they would chase him away whey they realized he had so little education. 'I was actually trembling with fear,' says Sammy, 'but they welcomed me and allowed me to take part.'

Following Sammy's appeal for help, Wycliffe translators Iver and Alice Larson from Denmark went to live among the Sabaot to learn their language. Sammy helped Iver to analyse the spoken language. An alphabet was produced, rules of grammar identified, literacy classes started, and, after some time, they translated the Gospel of Mark into Sabaot.

When the printed booklet of Mark arrived on the mountain, Sammy couldn't wait to show it to the chief. He said, 'I know my name is not on this book but I have helped write it. It is part of the Bible in our language.'

Today the Sabaot people have the whole New Testament. God is speaking to them in their own language. They can understand his words and know that he hears and loves the Sabaot people.

Like Sammy, there are many other people whose names are not on the book but who have helped to write God's words on the hearts of the Sabaot Christians: Jim and Henny Leonard, Francis Kiboi and Kiboki Kigai have all played a part in this story (see more about them

> *Sammy decided to walk the 100 miles to the meeting*

below). There are many others whose names don't even get into this article: those who provided administrative back-up in Nairobi, USA and Britain; those who provided prayer, encouragement and the funds necessary for the task.

The Sabaot New Testament was completed by Bible Translation and Literacy—or BTL—the Kenyan organization that now oversees all the translation projects in Kenya. Wycliffe members continue to work alongside Kenyan colleagues in this and many other projects. Around the world, Wycliffe is equipping the speakers of about 1,000 different languages with God's word and the skills to read it. But over 3,000 languages still do not have even a single word of the Bible.

Wycliffe's vision is that a Bible translation programme will have started in every language that still needs one by the year 2025. You can find out more at www.wycliffe.org.uk or by writing to Wycliffe Bible Translators, Horsleys Green, High Wycombe, Bucks HP14 3XL.

The long road to the Sabaot New Testament

1949   Sabaot men educated in English and Swahili begin work on putting their own language into a written form.

1953   The team reaches a conclusion: 'This language can never be written. It can only be spoken.'

1978–79 After a plea to the Bible Society of Kenya, members of Wycliffe Bible Translators conduct a language survey of Sabaot.

1981   Wycliffe members and people from the Sabaot community form a new translation team. Study of the language confirms that it cannot be written down—at least, not using the five vowels used in Kiswahili. Sabaot has twenty vowels, thirteen consonants and a complicated tonal system. A new alphabet is developed and accepted by the Kenyan Institute of Education.

1987   Excitement as the first translated book in Sabaot, Mark's Gospel, is published. One local pastor says, 'Before, God was far away, but now it is as if Jesus is walking here on this mountain.'

1990	Luke's Gospel is dedicated. The District Commissioner comments that 'the Word of God is the key to development in our community'.
1991	Jim and Henry Leonard, from the USA, take over as Project Leaders. The Larsens continue as consultants, and the Leonards and the Sabaot project staff proceed to translate even faster.
1994	The Leonards return to Nairobi, and Francis Kiboi assumes leadership of the project.
1996	Under the leadership of Kiboki Kigai, the New Testament receives its final check and is officially finished. After being typeset in Nairobi, it is sent to Dallas to produce the printing plates. Then it's on its way to South Korea to be printed.
1997	One year later, the printed New Testament arrives in Nairobi. At the official dedication on Sunday 14 December, close to 1,000 copies are bought.
2000	A dramatized version of the New Testament is recorded in Sabaot by the organization 'Faith Comes by Hearing'.
2002	A seven-member team is working to complete the Old Testament and to ensure that the Sabaot are capable of reading the scriptures and applying them to their daily lives. The plan is to complete the whole Bible by the year 2008.

Bible translation does take time but most don't take quite this long. The average time (for translations finishing today) is 10 to 15 years. Advances in technology, higher levels of partnership and an increased number of trained nationals are speeding up the process dramatically.

Peter Brassington has worked in various areas of mission, and is now a writer with Wycliffe, encouraging UK Christians to get involved in world mission.

BRF's Trustees

Graham Usher

As a child, the scenery at the annual Christmas pantomime always fascinated me. At the Theatre Royal in York, the stage sets were totally over the top and I was intrigued by watching them move in from the wings or come down on pulleys from above the stage. There was always some kind of scene like the laundry in *Aladdin*, where various parts of the scenery would move and spurt water so that by the end of the day's washing everyone was totally soaked. You got a glimpse behind the scenes of what you imagined might go on in an everyday laundry!

Organizations can be similar. We all have our ideas about how an organization works and we can often put a thick gloss of awe and wonder on to it. The reality is that so often they are run by ordinary people doing extraordinary things with limited resources.

At BRF the greatest asset, to my mind, is the staff team that we have. We know that many of you appreciate the service that you receive from BRF and we are conscious that the sense of BRF's 'fellowship' needs to cover all of our activities. Also serving BRF is a group of trustees—laity and clergy from a range of backgrounds and Church traditions. We form the Council, which meets twice a year for a full day as the policy-making body of BRF. With an organization that is 81 years old, the sense of history lies on our shoulders and

we have a responsibility to remember the founding aims of BRF.

In recent years, among other things, the Council has spent time looking at how the Church will develop in the next two decades and the particular trends that we may face. This has implications for how we can reach more people with our Bible reading notes, and how our branding and marketing needs to sit alongside these changes.

In all of its work, the Council looks to discern God's will for BRF. We meet within the context of prayer and the study of the scriptures: each meeting begins with a Council member sharing a portion of scripture with the group.

The twice-yearly Council meeting is not, however, the only requirement of the trustees. A number of us form the Business

Management Committee—in a sense, BRF's executive committee—that oversees the day-to-day management in conjunction with Richard Fisher, the Chief Executive, and senior staff. This group meets bi-monthly in Oxford and is very much at the forefront of planning and implementing, reviewing and monitoring the work.

In many ways we are quite a close family, developing deep friendships, and this, I hope, plays out in the way that the staff feel supported in their work. All of the trustees are committed to pray daily for BRF and our staff team.

Any involvement with a publishing house requires the trustees to read much material. We are often sent extracts from manuscripts for comment, and our bookshelves fill up with BRF titles. Most of us are avid readers in the religious market anyway and we are keen to read what other publishers are producing, as well as visiting Christian bookshops to look at new themes and titles, and to gauge how BRF books are placed on the shelves!

A recent exciting development within BRF has been our ministry to the Church at large. Our work with adults has been a source of huge blessing and we are conscious of the important work in reaching people through retreats, quiet days and seminars. This, of course, is a useful way to promote BRF's publications, but it also goes back to the founding vision of supporting Christians in their pilgrimage with Jesus Christ. I have seen the transforming power of this first-hand at quiet days that have been run in my inner-city parish in Middlesbrough, which have done much to introduce folk to the daily reading of the Bible.

At the heart of BRF is a passion for making the Bible come alive for all God's people

We are committed also to introducing children and young people to the Bible from an early age and allowing them to wallow, with a guiding hand, in the texts that we treasure. It has been a joy for me to take some of the newly published Barnabas books to the school where I am a governor. They also get field-tested at home on my young son at bedtime!

At the heart of BRF is a passion for making the Bible come alive for all God's people. For me, many of the resources that we produce make the Bible as exciting as the height of a pantomime's fun and games. I am lucky that from my seat I can see much of the workings behind the scenes as well.

An extract from
The Music of Praise

This book presents 52 meditations on well-known hymns from 'Amazing Grace' to 'When I Survey the Wondrous Cross'. Author Gordon Giles, whose work involves musical and liturgical responsibilities at St Paul's Cathedral, explores the meaning of the words, the beauty of the music, and their relevance for people today. The book is also a journey through the Christian year with the hymn writers and musicians who have sustained the faith of millions yesterday and today.

When I survey the wondrous cross
on which the Prince of glory died,
my richest gain I count but loss,
and pour contempt on all my pride.

Forbid it, Lord, that I should boast,
save in the death of Christ my God:
all the vain things that charm me most,
I sacrifice them to his blood.

See from his head, his hands, his feet,
sorrow and love flow mingled down:
did e'er such love and sorrow meet,
or thorns compose so rich a crown.

His dying crimson, like a robe
Spreads o'er his body on the Tree;
Then am I dead to all the globe,
And all the globe is dead to me.

Were the whole realm of nature mine,
that were a present far too small;
love so amazing, so divine,
demands my soul, my life, my all.

WORDS: ISAAC WATTS (1674–1748)
TUNE: 'ROCKINGHAM', EDWARD MILLER (1731–1807), ADAPTED FROM PSALM TUNES COLLECTED BY SAMUEL WEBBE THE YOUNGER (1770–1843)

Like Samuel Crossman's 'My song is love unknown', this hymn draws its inspiration from St Paul's words to the Galatians: 'May I never boast of anything except the cross of our Lord Jesus Christ, by which the world has been crucified to me, and I to the world' (Galatians 6:14).

Here Isaac Watts speaks of being 'dead to the globe', but it is effectively a direct quotation, as is the opening of the second verse, 'Forbid it, Lord, that I should boast, Save in the death of Christ my God'. This hymn has a clear scriptural basis, and at the same time offers a reflection upon it, rather as a preacher might comment. Watts draws us in: 'See, from his hands...'. He invites us to examine the Passion of Jesus, and yet does so in a way that maintains his own humility and thus encourages our own. The emotional impact of this hymn is unmistakable, and this may account for its tremendous popularity over a great many years.

Like a lot of good seasonal hymns, though, it is rarely sung for more than one week of the year. This is a shame, because the cross of Christ lies at the heart of all our worship, and Isaac Watts never intended it to be solely a Passiontide hymn. He wrote it for a collection of 1707, and designated it as a communion hymn, to be sung on any day, during or immediately after the distribution of bread and wine... Watts uses the image of blood and wine when he talks of love and sorrow flowing, mingled, down, and this reminds us of the blood and water flowing from Jesus' side after he had died on the cross (John 19:34).

For some, the fourth verse is too graphic in this respect. It tells of Jesus' 'dying crimson', spreading like a garment over the cross, blood pouring from wounded limbs. It is a gory image, but one which, like some of the more grotesque pictures of Christ by Mathias Grünewald (1480-1528), represents a painful reality. And yet, in that depiction of horrible death, there is the overtone of life-

not just the simple idea that Christ died that we might live, but also the idea that the 'Tree' referred to by Watts is also the Tree of Life. The cross of shame, an embarrassment and a foolish thing to Gentiles, becomes the tree of life, bearing the fruit of forgiveness, redemption and eternal life. The fourth verse may be bloody, but it is one of the most important verses, and contains, of course, the direct quotation from St Paul on which the hymn is based.

It is easy to see, then, why this communion hymn has been taken to the very heart of English-speaking Passiontide spirituality. All the elements are there, beginning with the intrinsic value of the crucifixion for our salvation... We stand with Watts, with the whole globe even, at the foot of the cross, and we cast aside all the vain things that might prevent us fully understanding and feeling what our Lord has done for us. Thus as we stand there, weak and humble before Christ's sacrifice, we are on solid ground biblically. This is no soppy lament for the pain of the cross-this is theology living and breathing and bleeding. In few hymns or poems are love and sorrow held together so perfectly, both in the text and in the singer...

The final verse is the hardest in so many respects. At the end it demands everything of us. God's offering, or present, or gift of his only Son is such that we can only respond with all our human love, which hardly matches to the amazing divine love expressed in the giving of Jesus for the whole globe. Watts referred to this love as a 'present', although some translations have rendered it as 'offering', just in case anyone misses the point!

This hymn is not so popular just because of its words, though. The tune Rockingham, to which it is invariably sung in Britain and elsewhere, is an exquisitely lyrical, flowing tune, which illustrates that love and sorrow, flowing, mingled, down. Words and music mingle, and we are slowly but surely swept along on a gentle tide of contemplation and worship. The major key is used, perhaps surprisingly, but therefore with greater effect. There is no lugubriousness here, no wallowing in the minor key as we sing of what a shame it is that Christ died. This old and famous hymn tune does not want to say that, or make us say it; it wants us to boast in the death of Christ, because of the victory to which it leads. And yet this is not a proud tune either. The triumph of the cross is muted, and the direction of the hymn is not outward: we are telling it abroad, but rather internalizing our meditation on the suffering and the glory of the cross.

There is a form of meditation advocated by St Ignatius of Loyola, known as the Spiritual Exercises, which, if followed properly, brings us to the foot of the cross in the third week. Ignatius is most often associated with the Roman Catholic Jesuits, but the idea of cross-centred meditation, in which one imagines oneself as being present, is an ancient tradition that has continued to develop. Richard Baxter, a Puritan with whom Watts was in sympathy, wrote a work in 1657 entitled The Crucifying of the World for the Cross of Christ, in which he too employed this kind of imaginative technique. Edward Miller's version of the old Psalm tune sets a contemplative tone, which further encourages us to imagine the realities of the crucifixion scene, yet without pretentiousness or self-deception.

This ideal marriage of tune and words was not brought about until 1833, when a version of Tallis' Canon was abandoned as the tune in favour of Miller's arrangement, which he named after the Marquis of Rockingham, a personal friend and three-times Prime Minister of Great Britain. Although the tune had been set to other psalms previously, it settled down to its current position, and now it is hard to imagine any other tune fitting these words more successfully, nor this tune being used for any other hymn.

This is an abridged extract from the chapter for the Second Week of Lent in The Music of Praise. *To order a copy of the book, please turn to page 159.*

An extract from
On the Way to Calvary

In this book, Hilary McDowell's third for BRF, we follow the path of the 'traveller', first met in Hilary's Advent book *On the Way to Bethlehem* (BRF, 1998). Although rooted in the 21st century, she journeys alongside Jesus to the cross and beyond to the joy of an empty tomb, in the company of many Bible characters. Her discoveries sometimes astound her, sometimes empower her, but always challenge her to learn lessons for life today.

Temptations in the Desert

Then Jesus was led up by the spirit into the wilderness to be tempted by the devil. And he fasted forty days and forty nights, and afterward he was hungry. And the tempter came and said to him. 'If you are the Son of God, command these stones to become loaves of bread.' But he answered, 'It is written, Man shall not live by bread alone, but by every word that proceeds from the mouth of God' (Matthew 4:14)

Feeling like an experienced traveller, on this journey she travelled light. The knapsack hopped up and down on her back, with little weight to retain it, as she jogged towards Jerusalem.

Slowly the terrain changed. Great stretches of sunflower fields had given way to a rising gradient and a distant circle of hills gradually crept nearer. She was going 'up' to Jerusalem.

Maybe I could carry something up this hill for him, she thought, turning full circle to see where he was. But she was alone. The realization shook her somewhat. 'I thought you invited me to talk with you,' she shouted to the silent hills. The low drone of a passing insect was the only reply. She sat down by the side of the dirt path and waited. All day she waited and all night too, shivering beneath the flimsy covering she had packed....

By first light she removed the Bible from her knapsack, grateful to have something to consult. 'Where would he be?' she muttered to herself as she leafed through the well-thumbed pages. 'Where did he go first?' Backwards her fingers flipped, before Holy Week, before even his three years of recorded ministry... ah, here it is, she thought—the wilderness! He spent forty days in the wilderness. Now all she had to do was negotiate her compass and maps to locate the desert. 'Shouldn't be too difficult,' she mused, 'in this country.' Sand, rocks, sand and more sand... now where would he be?

By nightfall huge craggy pinnacles of rock towered above her, pitted with holes gorged in their sides... Gratefully she headed for one of these caves to shelter for the night. All through the hours of darkness, strange animal cries punctuated her sleep. Her fitful rest was unsatisfying and she awakened feeling bruised and stiff. A rock bed was no substitute for her Laura Ashley covers. Home seemed suddenly so alluring.

The temperature rose steeply the next day and shelter became more scarce. She knelt by a parched, stubby bush and prayed. 'Dear God, I know your Son is here somewhere, but I don't really think it's good for anyone to stay too long in this terrain. My head feels really dizzy with the heat, and the more dehydrated I become, the less able I am to think straight. Couldn't you just take us both on a little faster? To tell the truth, I wouldn't mind skipping this part of the journey altogether. I don't really need to be here at all, you know. I have a good life at home—well, most of the time. Food is plentiful and my house is a great improvement on your average cave. I only came to apply the benefit of my 21st-century experience to your Son's present predicament. I'd like to minister to his needs, you see. I follow him as best I can and it really concerns me what he is going through here, so if you could just—

Stopped in mid-sentence by an unexpected cool breeze across her temples, she opened her eyes to see the outline of a man moving about fifty yards to her right. Covered in the characteristic robes of the nomadic tribesmen of that region, his body slightly stooped, the man pushed forward into a desert wind which had now turned hot and stifling. His hand held part of the clothing across his mouth against the flying dust and grit of the wilderness. She somehow knew it was *him*. It shocked her to see how insignificant he looked against the backdrop of the surrounding terrain.

Quickening her step, she drew alongside him. 'Lord,' she urged, 'please, Lord, slow down a little. We have plenty of time.' His progress continued as before. Without stopping, she removed her flask and held it out to him. 'Have a sip, Master. You must be thirsty.' As he strode onwards, eyes fixed ahead, steps unwavering, she realized that she was unseen... So she could only observe, not dwell in this century. What a disappointment! She could not help him, then. She fell behind a step, gutted by the realization, and, determined to return home, she rested on the ground. Then she remembered the plain card in the kitchen drawer. 'Come to Calvary.' Well, she was on the way and it must be for a reason, so she would continue.

Looking up in search of the lone figure, her eyes scanned ahead and there, about a hundred yards into the sun, two people seemed to be striding side by side. It was him all right, but now he was not alone. She ran to catch up and paced a little behind, overhearing their conversation. The other man seemed to be trying to help him also; in a concerned and empathetic tone he was holding something out to the Lord and urging him to eat. So she wasn't the only one with his concerns at heart, she thought. For a moment she experienced a surge of relief to know that someone from his own time was there to help. But the relief only lasted a brief moment.

As she drew close enough to see clearly against the glare of the sun, she was able to identify what the stranger held in his hand. It was a stone. She wanted to cry out a warning. She longed to grab that stone from the tempter's hand and fling it to the desert floor. She felt the fear of the dark presence of the stranger flood over her soul, threatening to swamp her resolve. The evil one was coaxing Jesus now. 'If you are the son of God,' he flattered, 'command these stones to become loaves of bread.'

Suddenly it jolted all her annual Lenten fasting into proportion. It made a mockery of her mixed motives—to be able to fit into the summer bikini… Hunger, real hunger, was gnawing at her insides. Exhaustion, dehydration, and fear of never finding the next meal, threatened her survival. Her befuddled, heat-oppressed brain conjured up images of unanswered needs at home—her life's fears for her family, her job, her health, and the loneliness of modern living, surrounded though she was at home by a myriad of people.

In an instant she would have snatched that stone and begged the Lord to let it materialize into the love she longed for, the break from routine she craved, the freedom from her heavy responsibilities, the— Pulling herself into focus again, she recognized the endless lists of needs and drives and heart's desires that were now flooding her consciousness like harpies rushing her to destruction. With a giant renewed focus upon her Master just a few feet away, she pushed aside all thoughts in time to hear him say, 'Man shall not live by bread alone, but by every word that proceeds from the mouth of God.'

The bad one fell back a step or two as though a physical blow had been dealt, yet no punch had been thrown. As the two figures moved on together across the parched ground, she sank to her knees, reaching shaky hands out to God in prayer…

This is an abridged extract from the reading for Ash Wednesday in On the Way to Calvary. *To order a copy of the book, please turn to page 159.*

The People's Bible Commentary

The book of 1 Corinthians describes the problems and challenges facing a young church. Paul wrote his letter to help the Corinthian Christians live out their faith in one of the largest and most notorious cities in the ancient world, and his words still resonate in our culture today. Author Jerome Murphy-O'Connor is Professor of New Testament at the École Biblique in Jerusalem.

1 CORINTHIANS 13:1–3

LOVING IS BEING

The tradition of classical rhetoric, in which Paul was trained, advised a 'digression' in the course of a complex development. It was a trick to win the goodwill of the audience by giving them a momentary break from the concentration needed to follow the argument. It was also a moment when the speaker/writer was encouraged to give his talent full rein in order to delight and relax his audience. The only condition was that there had to be some connection with the matter under discussion.

What Paul does in this celebrated 'Hymn to Love' perfectly illustrates not only his knowledge of the rules of rhetoric, but the perfection of his technique. Although there are subtle links to the spiritual gifts, the topic is different, and his language soars rhythmically. He shifts our perspective to a fundamental theme that underlies the whole thrust of this letter.

Gifts without love

The digression opens with three statements all constructed on the same pattern, 'If I have... but have not love, I am...'. The abrupt shift to the first person singular reinforces the dramatic rhythm of the repetition. No one hearing the letter read aloud could be unaware that something new was going on, even if the reader was not very good. Yet there are echoes of what Paul has just been speaking about in that love is contrasted with spiritual gifts.

The fact that Paul mentions first

'the tongues of men and of angels' indicates once again that the gift of speaking in tongues is at the top of his agenda in this part of the letter. The natural sense of 'tongues of men' is foreign languages (Paul's education would have made him familiar with Hebrew, Aramaic, and Greek), but 'tongues of angels' can only be speech that is unintelligible to humans. When pronounced without care for others, it resembles 'sounding brass'. Stone theatres did not enhance the actors' voices by resonance, as the older wooden theatres had done. To compensate, brass vases were located at strategic points. They were turned upside down and tilted open towards the stage by wedges. When tuned, they contributed a resonant hum that gave body to the actors' voices, but was in itself unintelligible.

The other spiritual gifts evoked by Paul are prophecy, knowledge, and faith, all of which appear in 12:8–10. The relation of faith to moving mountains reflects Paul's knowledge of the teaching of Jesus, 'If you have faith as a grain of mustard see, you will say to this mountain, "Move hence to yonder place," and it will move' (Matthew 17:20; Mark 11:23).

The gift of 'helping' (12:28) is dramatized in rendering oneself destitute in order to help another, and in the acceptance of a supremely painful death in a great cause. Yet both are barren gestures, if they are not inspired by love.

Without love I am nothing

The most fundamental statement in this opening section of the 'Hymn to Love' is 'without love I am nothing' (13:2). This should not be read as if it were the equivalent of 'I am useless'. Paul means that without love we do not exist. In other words, we come into being through loving. Paul here diverges radically from every philosophical view of human nature. He took seriously the revelation of Christ. In giving himself for us Christ revealed that true humanity consisted in loving (Galatians 2:20). Loving is what makes a person genuinely human.

Love, however, must have as its object another person. Thus, A exists as human and as Christian only in loving B. One cannot be a completely isolated Christian. There must always be an active reference to at least one other person. Here we find the profound reason why Paul had to think of the Church in terms of an organic unity such as the human body. The lover and the beloved share a common existence in precisely the same way as the arm and the leg co-exist.

Prayer
Lord, give me the gift of loving.

To order a copy of this book, please turn to page 159.

All we need is Love

Kaye Johnson

'Ouch, that hurt!' cried Pain.

'There's not enough room in here. Please can you give me some space?' asked Isolation.

'I don't like the dark,' whimpered Fear.

There was such a commotion and confusion in the cupboard, pushing and shoving, each one trying to take charge over the others. Fear was the most dominant, but on the odd occasion Pain would take over, while Isolation kept quiet in the corner, as far away from the others as possible. Hate, you see, had locked them in the cupboard and wouldn't let them out.

Being crammed into such a tiny place was causing such turmoil, yet they were all so focused on gaining control that they didn't notice the little girl curled up in a ball, rocking herself. At least, they didn't notice her till she let out a sigh of defeat.

'What's wrong with you?' snapped Fear.

'My mum has locked me in the cupboard because I made a big mistake. I forgot to put enough sugar in her tea.'

'Is that all?' said Fear. 'Well, we have been locked in here by Hate, and I'm so scared.'

'You always are,' sniffed Pain.

'My mum was very angry,' went on the little girl.

'I know some Anger,' said the quiet voice of Isolation. 'I wonder if it's the same one?'

'Anger? Oh, I know him, he won't leave me alone! He's a bully. I just don't know what I did to upset him but he always seems to be wherever I am. I'm scared of him!' said Fear, his voice a little quivery.

'Is there anything you're not scared of?' asked Pain sarcastically. 'You think you're so much in control, but you're not. I'm stronger than you,' Fear barked at Pain.

'Please,' said the little girl. 'Please don't argue.'

'That's why I prefer to be alone,' said Isolation. 'They're always at it, each trying to better the other. What they don't seem to realize is that they are both equals, and that really, although I'm embarrassed to admit it, really I'm the greatest of us all. I do try to hide the fact, as I'm not proud of it.'

Well, here I am locked in a cupboard with Isolation, Fear and Pain, thought the little girl. So why do I feel so alone? I do wish they would all stop fighting!

'OUCH! Now that was my foot,' sobbed Pain.

'You shouldn't have made me jump, then,' shrieked Fear.

'Well, you—' but before Pain could finish, the little girl started to cry.

'Oh, don't cry,' whispered Isolation. 'We are all here with you—Pain, Fear and myself. We won't leave you, so don't worry.'

'Don't worry! What do you mean, "Don't worry"?' cried Fear. 'She's got everything to worry about. We are all going to die in here, we are just going to rot!'

'The very thought of it hurts,' sobbed Pain.

'I'm quite happy in here,' said Isolation.

'Well, I'm not. I can't even begin to think how I'm going to get out. Now I'm really scared,' wept Fear.

'Please just shut up,' said Pain coldly.

There was a deadly silence in the cupboard. Isolation moved further into the corner, Fear covered his face with his hands, Pain curled up into a ball, and the little girl sighed another sigh of defeat.

After what seemed like an eternity of silence, the little girl said in a very small whisper, 'Does any one know Love?'

'No,' said Isolation. 'I've heard of him but never met him.'

'Me neither,' chorused Pain and Fear.

'Didn't your mother introduce you to him?' asked Isolation.

'No,' said the little girl. 'She couldn't find him either.'

'I heard that Hate can't bear to be in the same room as Love,' said Pain.

'Then that's the answer!' cried Fear. 'We need Love!'

There was silence again in the cupboard, as none of them knew how to find Love or even where to start looking. Nobody knew what he looked like. The little girl placed her head upon her knees and waited.

Kaye Johnson lives with her son in a small seaside town in Kent, as part of a very busy vicarage household. She started writing as she found it a way of healing.

New Daylight © BRF 2003

The Bible Reading Fellowship
First Floor, Elsfield Hall, 15–17 Elsfield Way, Oxford OX2 8FG
ISBN 1 84101 039 1

Distributed in Australia by:
Willow Connection, PO Box 288, Brookvale, NSW 2100.
Tel: 02 9948 3957; Fax: 02 9948 8153;
E-mail: info@willowconnection.com.au
Available also from all good Christian bookshops in Australia.
For individual and group subscriptions in Australia:
Mrs Rosemary Morrall, PO Box W35, Wanniassa, ACT 2903.

Distributed in New Zealand by:
Scripture Union Wholesale, PO Box 760, Wellington
Tel: 04 385 0421; Fax: 04 384 3990; E-mail: suwholesale@clear.net.nz

Distributed in South Africa by:
Struik Book Distributors, PO Box 193, Maitland 7405, Cape Town
Tel: 021 551 5900; Fax: 021 551 1124; E-mail: enquiries@struik.co.za

Distributed in the USA by:
The Bible Reading Fellowship, PO Box 380, Winter Park,
Florida 32790-0380
Tel: 407 628 4330 or 800 749 4331; Fax: 407 647 2406;
E-mail: brf@biblereading.org; Website: www.biblereading.org

Publications distributed to more than 60 countries

Acknowledgments
The New Revised Standard Version of the Bible, Anglicized Edition, copyright © 1989, 1995 by the
Division of Christian Education of the National Council of the Churches of Christ in the USA.
Used by permission. All rights reserved.

The Holy Bible, New International Version, copyright © 1973, 1978, 1984 by International Bible
Society. Used by permission of Hodder & Stoughton Limited. All rights reserved. 'NIV' is a
registered trademark of International Bible Society. UK trademark number 1448790.

The New Jerusalem Bible, published and copyright © 1985 by Darton, Longman and Todd Ltd and
les Editions du Cerf, and by Doubleday, a division of Bantam Doubleday Dell Publishing Group, Inc.
Used by permission of Darton, Longman and Todd Ltd, and Doubleday, a division of Random
House, Inc.

The New King James Bible copyright © 1979, 1980. 1982 by Thomas Nelson, Inc. Used by
permission. All rights reserved.

The Contemporary English Version, copyright © American Bible Society 1991, 1992, 1995. Used by
permission/Anglicizations copyright © British and Foreign Bible Society 1997.

Extracts from The Book of Common Prayer of 1662, the rights of which are vested in the Crown in
perpetuity within the United Kingdom, are reproduced by permission of Cambridge University
Press, Her Majesty's Printers.

The Revised Common Lectionary is copyright © The Consultation on Common Texts, 1992 and is
reproduced with permission. *The Christian Year: Calendar, Lectionary and Collects*, which includes the
Common Worship lectionary (the Church of England's adaptations of the *Revised Common Lectionary*,
published as the Principal Service lectionary) is copyright © The Central Board of Finance of the
Church of England, 1995, 1997, and material from it is reproduced with permission.

Printed in Denmark

BRF seeks to help people of all ages to experience the living God—Father, Son and Holy Spirit—at a deeper level, and enable them to grow as disciples of Jesus Christ through the Bible, prayer and worship.

We need your help if we are to make a real impact on the local church and community. In an increasingly secular world people need even more help with their Bible reading, their prayer and their discipleship. We can do something about this, but our resources are limited. With your help, if we all do a little, together we can make a huge difference.

How can you help?

- You could become a *Friend of BRF* and encourage BRF's ministry within your own church and community (contact the BRF office, or visit the BRF website, www.brf.org.uk).

- You could support BRF's ministry with a donation or standing order (using the response form overleaf).

- You could consider making a bequest to BRF in your will, and so give lasting support to our work. (We have a leaflet available with more information about this, which can be requested using the form overleaf.)

- And, most important of all, you could become a BRF *Prayer Partner* and support BRF with your prayers. *Prayer Partners* receive our bi-monthly prayer letter which includes details of all that is going on within BRF and specific prayer pointers for each prayer need. (To become a *Prayer Partner* write to Jane Usher at BRF or e-mail jane.usher@brf.org.uk)

Whatever you can do or give, we thank you for your support.

BRF MINISTRY APPEAL RESPONSE FORM

Name _____

Address _____

_____ Postcode _____

Telephone _____ Email _____

(tick as appropriate)

Gift Aid Declaration

☐ I am a UK taxpayer. I want BRF to treat as Gift Aid Donations all donations I make from the date of this declaration until I notify you otherwise.

Signature _____ Date _____

☐ I would like to support BRF's ministry with a regular donation by standing order (please complete the Banker's Order below).

Standing Order – Banker's Order

To the Manager, Name of Bank/Building Society _____

Address _____

_____ Postcode _____

Sort Code _____ Account Name _____

Account No _____

Please pay Royal Bank of Scotland plc, London Drummonds Branch, 49 Charing Cross, London SW1A 2DX (Sort Code 16-00-38), for the account of BRF A/C No. 00774151

The sum of _____ pounds on ___ / ___ / ___ (insert date your standing order starts) and thereafter the same amount on the same day of each month until further notice.

Signature _____ Date _____

Single donation

☐ I enclose my cheque/credit card/Switch card details for a donation of

£5 £10 £25 £50 £100 £250 (other) £ _____ to support BRF's ministry

Credit/ Switch card no. ☐☐☐☐☐☐☐☐☐☐☐☐☐☐☐☐☐☐☐

Expires ☐☐ ☐☐   Issue no. of Switch card ☐☐☐

Signature _____ Date _____

(Where appropriate, on receipt of your donation, we will send you a Gift Aid form)

☐ Please send me information about making a bequest to BRF in my will.

Please detach and send this completed form to: Richard Fisher, BRF, First Floor, Elsfield Hall, 15–17 Elsfield Way, Oxford OX2 8FG. BRF is a Registered Charity (No.233280)

NEW DAYLIGHT SUBSCRIPTIONS

Please note our subscription rates 2003–2004. From the May 2003 issue, the new subscription rates will be:

Individual subscriptions covering 3 issues for under 5 copies, payable in advance (including postage and packing):

	UK	SURFACE	AIRMAIL
NEW DAYLIGHT each set of 3 p.a.	£11.10	£12.45	£14.70
NEW DAYLIGHT 3-year sub i.e. 9 issues	£27.45	N/A	N/A
(Not available for Large Print)			
NEW DAYLIGHT LGE PRINT each set of 3 p.a.	£16.80	£20.40	£24.90

Group subscriptions covering 3 issues for 5 copies or more, sent to ONE address (post free):

NEW DAYLIGHT	£9.15	each set of 3 p.a.
NEW DAYLIGHT LGE PRINT	£14.97	each set of 3 p.a.

Please note that the annual billing period for Group Subscriptions runs from 1 May to 30 April.

Copies of the notes may also be obtained from Christian bookshops:

NEW DAYLIGHT	£3.05 each copy
NEW DAYLIGHT LGE PRINT	£4.99 each copy

NEW DAYLIGHT SUBSCRIPTIONS

❏ I would like to give a gift subscription (please complete both name and address sections below)

❏ I would like to take out a subscription myself (complete name and address details only once)

This completed coupon should be sent with appropriate payment to BRF. Alternatively, please write to us quoting your name, address, the subscription you would like for either yourself or a friend (with their name and address), the start date and credit card number, expiry date and signature if paying by credit card.

Gift subscription name _____

Gift subscription address _____

_____

_____ Postcode _____

Please send beginning with the May/September 2003/January 2004 issue: (delete as applicable)

(please tick box)	UK	SURFACE	AIR MAIL
NEW DAYLIGHT	❏ £11.10	❏ £12.45	❏ £14.70
NEW DAYLIGHT 3-year sub	❏ £27.45		
NEW DAYLIGHT LARGE PRINT	❏ £16.80	❏ £20.40	❏ £24.90

Please complete the payment details below and send your coupon, with appropriate payment to: **BRF, First Floor, Elsfield Hall, 15–17 Elsfield Way, Oxford OX2 8FG.**

Your name _____

Your address _____

_____

_____ Postcode _____

Total enclosed £ _____ (cheques should be made payable to 'BRF')

Payment by cheque ❏ postal order ❏ Visa ❏ Mastercard ❏ Switch ❏

Card number: ❏❏❏❏❏❏❏❏❏❏❏❏❏❏❏❏❏❏

Expiry date of card: ❏❏❏❏   Issue number (Switch): ❏❏❏❏

Signature (essential if paying by credit/Switch card) _____

❏ Please send me further information about BRF publications

ND0103   BRF is a Registered Charity

Please ensure that you complete and send off both sides of this order form.

Please send me the following book(s):

		Quantity	Price	Total
3552 4	When You Walk (A. Plass)	_____	£7.99	_____
126 6	Living the Gospel (Helen Julian CSF)	_____	£5.99	_____
212 2	Still Time for Eternity (M. Cundiff)	_____	£5.99	_____
222 X	Feasting on God's Word (D. Spriggs)	_____	£6.99	_____
237 8	The Music of Praise (G. Giles)	_____	£12.99	_____
243 2	The Gospels Unplugged (L. Moore)	_____	£12.99	_____
249 1	On the Way to Calvary (H. McDowell)	_____	£6.99	_____
324 2	With Jesus in the Upper Room (D. Winter)	_____	£12.99	_____

People's Bible Commentary

		Quantity	Price	Total
030 8	PBC: 1 & 2 Samuel (H. Mowvley)	_____	£7.99	_____
118 5	PBC: 1 & 2 Kings (S. Dawes)	_____	£7.99	_____
070 7	PBC: Chronicles—Nehemiah (M. Tunnicliffe)	_____	£7.99	_____
094 4	PBC: Job (K. Dell)	_____	£7.99	_____
031 6	PBC: Psalms 1—72 (D. Coggan)	_____	£7.99	_____
065 0	PBC: Psalms 73—150 (D. Coggan)	_____	£7.99	_____
071 5	PBC: Proverbs (E. Mellor)	_____	£7.99	_____
087 1	PBC: Jeremiah (R. Mason)	_____	£7.99	_____
040 5	PBC: Ezekiel (E. Lucas)	_____	£7.99	_____
028 6	PBC: Nahum—Malachi (G. Emmerson)	_____	£7.99	_____
191 6	PBC: Matthew (J. Proctor)	_____	£7.99	_____
046 4	PBC: Mark (D. France)	_____	£7.99	_____
027 8	PBC: Luke (H. Wansbrough)	_____	£7.99	_____
029 4	PBC: John (R.A. Burridge)	_____	£7.99	_____
082 0	PBC: Romans (J. Dunn)	_____	£7.99	_____
122 3	PBC: 1 Corinthians (J. Murphy-O'Connor)	_____	£7.99	_____
073 1	PBC: 2 Corinthians (A. Besançon Spencer)	_____	£7.99	_____
012 X	PBC: Galatians and 1 & 2 Thessalonians (J. Fenton)	_____	£7.99	_____
047 2	PBC: Ephesians—Colossians & Philemon (M. Maxwell)	_____	£7.99	_____
119 3	PBC: Timothy, Titus and Hebrews (D. France)	_____	£7.99	_____
092 8	PBC: James—Jude (F. Moloney)	_____	£7.99	_____
3297 5	PBC: Revelation (M. Maxwell)	_____	£7.99	_____

Total cost of books £ _____

Postage and packing (see over) £ _____

TOTAL £ _____

See over for payment details. All prices are correct at time of going to press, are subject to the prevailing rate of VAT and may be subject to change without prior warning.

ND0103   The Bible Reading Fellowship is a Registered Charity

PAYMENT DETAILS

Please complete the payment details below and send with appropriate payment and completed order form to:

**BRF, First Floor, Elsfield Hall,
15–17 Elsfield Way, Oxford OX2 8FG**

Name _____

Address _____

_____

_____ Postcode _____

Telephone _____

Email _____

Total enclosed £ _____(cheques should be made payable to 'BRF')

Payment by cheque ❏ postal order ❏ Visa ❏ Mastercard ❏ Switch ❏

Card number: ⬚⬚⬚⬚⬚⬚⬚⬚⬚⬚⬚⬚⬚⬚⬚⬚⬚⬚⬚

Expiry date of card: ⬚⬚⬚⬚   Issue number (Switch): ⬚⬚⬚

Signature (essential if paying by credit/Switch card)_____

ALTERNATIVE WAYS TO ORDER

Christian bookshops: All good Christian bookshops stock BRF publications. For your nearest stockist, please contact BRF.

POSTAGE AND PACKING CHARGES				
order value	UK	Europe	Surface	Air Mail
£7.00 & under	£1.25	£3.00	£3.50	£5.50
£7.01–£30.00	£2.25	£5.50	£7.50	£11.50
Over £30.00	free	prices on request		

Telephone: The BRF office is open between 09.15 and 17.00.
To place your order, phone 01865 319700; fax 01865 319701.

❏ Please send me further information about BRF publications

Web: Visit www.brf.org.uk

BRF is a Registered Charity